PENGUIN BOOKS — GREAT IDEAS

*On Solitude*

Michel de Montaigne

1533–1592

# Michel de Montaigne

## *On Solitude*

TRANSLATED BY M. A. SCREECH

PENGUIN BOOKS — GREAT IDEAS

## PENGUIN BOOKS

Published by the Penguin Group
Penguin Books Ltd, 80 Strand, London WC2R ORL, England
Penguin Group (USA) Inc., 375 Hudson Street, New York, New York 10014, USA
Penguin Group (Canada), 90 Eglinton Avenue East, Suite 700, Toronto, Ontario,
Canada M4P 2Y3 (a division of Pearson Penguin Canada Inc.)
Penguin Ireland, 25 St Stephen's Green, Dublin 2, Ireland (a division of Penguin Books Ltd)
Penguin Group (Australia), 250 Camberwell Road, Camberwell, Victoria 3124, Australia
(a division of Pearson Australia Group Pty Ltd)
Penguin Books India Pvt Ltd, 11 Community Centre, Panchsheel Park,
New Delhi – 110 017, India
Penguin Group (NZ), 67 Apollo Drive, Rosedale, North Shore 0632, New Zealand
(a division of Pearson New Zealand Ltd)
Penguin Books (South Africa) (Pty) Ltd, 24 Sturdee Avenue, Rosebank, Johannesburg 2196,
South Africa

Penguin Books Ltd, Registered Offices: 80 Strand, London WC2R ORL, England

www.penguin.com

This translation first published in Penguin Classics 1991
This edition first published in Penguin Books 2009

010

Translation copyright © M. A. Screech 1991
All rights reserved

Set by Rowland Phototypesetting Ltd, Bury St Edmunds, Suffolk
Printed in England by Clays Ltd, Elcograf S.p.A.

ISBN: 978-0-141-39925-6

www.greenpenguin.co.uk

MIX
Paper from
responsible sources
FSC™ C018179

Penguin Books is committed to a sustainable
future for our business, our readers and our planet.
This book is made from Forest Stewardship
Council™ certified paper.

# Contents

# On Solitude

Let us leave aside those long comparisons between the solitary life and the active one; and as for that fine adage used as a cloak by greed and ambition, 'That we are not born for ourselves alone but for the common weal,'[1] let us venture to refer to those who have joined in the dance: let them bare their consciences and confess whether rank, office and all the bustling business of the world are not sought on the contrary to gain private profit from the common weal. The evil methods which men use to get ahead in our century clearly show that their aims cannot be worth much.

Let us retort to ambition that she herself gives us a taste for solitude, for does she shun anything more than fellowship? Does she seek anything more than room to use her elbows?

The means of doing good or evil can be found anywhere, but if that quip of Bias is true, that 'the evil form the larger part', or what Ecclesiasticus says, 'One good man in a thousand have I not found.'[2]

> *Rari quippe boni: numero vix sunt totidem, quot*
> *Thebarum portæ, vel divitis ostia Nili.*

1. Erasmus, *Adages*, IV, VI, VIII, *Nemo sibi nascitur*.
2. Ecclesiasticus 7:28; then, Juvenal, *Satires*, XIII, 26–7.

[Good men are rare: just about as many as gates in the walls of Thebes or mouths to the fertile Nile.]

then contagion is particularly dangerous in crowds. Either you must loathe the wicked or imitate them. It is dangerous both to grow like them because they are many, or to loathe many of them because they are different.

Sea-going merchants are right to ensure that dissolute, blasphemous or wicked men do not sail in the same ship with them, believing such company to be unlucky. That is why Bias jested with those who were going through the perils of a great storm with him and calling on the gods for help: 'Shut up,' he said, 'so that they do not realize that you are here with me.'[3] And (a more pressing example) when Albuquerque, the Viceroy of India for Emmanuel, King of Portugal, was in peril from a raging tempest, he took a boy on his shoulders for one reason only: so that by linking their fates together the innocence of that boy might serve him as a warrant and intercession for God's favour and so bring him to safety.

It is not that a wise man cannot live happily anywhere nor be alone in a crowd of courtiers, but Bias says that, if he has the choice, the wise man will avoid the very sight of them. If he has to, he will put up with the former, but if he can he will choose the other. He thinks that he is not totally free of vice if he has to contend with the vices of others.

3. Diogenes Laertius, *Life of Bias*.

Those who haunted evil-doers were chastised as evil by Charondas.[4]

There is nothing more unsociable than Man, and nothing more sociable: unsociable by his vice, sociable by his nature. And Antisthenes does not seem to me to have given an adequate reply to the person who reproached him for associating with the wicked, when he retorted that doctors live among the sick: for even if doctors do help the sick to return to health they impair their own by constantly seeing and touching diseases as they treat them.[5]

Now the end I think is always the same: how to live in leisure at our ease. But people do not always seek the way properly. Often they think they have left their occupations behind when they have merely changed them. There is hardly less torment in running a family than in running a whole country. Whenever our soul finds something to do she is there in her entirety: domestic tasks may be less important but they are no less importunate. Anyway, by ridding ourselves of Court and market-place we do not rid ourselves of the principal torments of our life:

> *ratio et prudentia curas,*
> *Non locus effusi late maris arbiter, aufert.*

[it is reason and wisdom which take away cares, not places affording wide views over the sea.][6]

4. Charondas the lawgiver of Sicily and follower of Pythagoras (Seneca, *Epist. moral.*, XC, 6).
5. Erasmus, *Apophthegmata*, VII, *Antisthenes Atheniensis*, XXII.
6. Horace, *Epistles*, I, xi, 25–6.

Ambition, covetousness, irresolution, fear and desires do not abandon us just because we have changed our landscape.

> *Et post equitem sedet atra cura.*
> [Behind the parting horseman squats black care.][7]

They often follow us into the very cloister and the schools of philosophy. Neither deserts nor holes in cliffs nor hair-shirts nor fastings can disentangle us from them:

> *haerit lateri letalis arundo.*
> [in her side still clings that deadly shaft.][8]

Socrates was told that some man had not been improved by travel. 'I am sure he was not,' he said. 'He went with himself!'[9]

> *Quid terras alio calentes*
> *Sole mutamus? patria quis exul*
> *Se quoque fugit?*
> [Why do we leave for lands warmed by a foreign sun? What fugitive from his own land can flee from himself?][10]

If you do not first lighten yourself and your soul of the weight of your burdens, moving about will only increase their pressure on you, as a ship's cargo is less troublesome

7. *Odes*, III, i, 40.    8. Virgil, *Aeneid*, IV, 73.
9. Seneca, *Epist. moral.*, CIV, 7, Erasmus, *Apophthegmata*, III, *Socrates*, XLIV.
10. Horace, *Odes*, II, xvi, 18–20.

when lashed in place. You do more harm than good to a patient by moving him about: you shake his illness down into the sack, just as you drive stakes in by pulling and waggling them about. That is why it is not enough to withdraw from the mob, not enough to go to another place: we have to withdraw from such attributes of the mob as are within us. It is our own self we have to isolate and take back into possession.

> *Rupi jam vincula dicas:*
> *Nam luctata canis nodum arripit; attamen illi,*
> *Cum fugit, a collo trahitur pars longa catenæ.*

['I have broken my chains,' you say. But a struggling cur may snap its chain, only to escape with a great length of it fixed to its collar.][11]

We take our fetters with us; our freedom is not total: we still turn our gaze towards the things we have left behind; our imagination is full of them.

> *Nisi purgatum est pectus, quæ prælia nobis*
> *Atque pericula tunc ingratis insinuandum?*
> *Quantæ conscindunt hominem cuppedinis acres*
> *Sollicitum curæ, quantique perinde timores?*
> *Quidve superbia, spurcitia, ac petulantia, quantas*
> *Efficiunt clades? quid luxus desidiesque?*

[But if our breast remains unpurged, what unprofitable battles and tempests we must face, what bitter cares must tear a man apart, and then what fears, what pride, what sordid thoughts,

11. Persius, *Satires*, V, 158–60.

what tempers and what clashes; what gross gratifications; what sloth!][12]

It is in our soul that evil grips us: and she cannot escape from herself:

*In culpa est animus qui se non effugit unquam.*
[That mind is at fault which never escapes from itself.][13]

So we must bring her back, haul her back, into our self. That is true solitude. It can be enjoyed in towns and in kings' courts, but more conveniently apart.

Now since we are undertaking to live, without companions, by ourselves, let us make our happiness depend on ourselves; let us loose ourselves from the bonds which tie us to others; let us gain power over ourselves to live really and truly alone – and of doing so in contentment.

Stilpo had escaped from the great conflagration of his city in which he had lost wife, children and goods; when Demetrius Poliorcetes saw him in the midst of so great a destruction of his homeland, yet with his face undismayed, he asked him if he had suffered no harm. He said, No. Thank God he had lost nothing of his.[14] The philosopher Antisthenes put the same thing amusingly when he said that a man ought to provide himself with unsinkable goods, which could float out of a shipwreck with him.[15]

12. Lucretius, V, 43–8.     13. Horace, *Epistles*, I, xiv, 13.
14. Seneca, *Epist. moral.*, IX, 18.
15. Diogenes Laertius, *Life of Antisthenes*.

Certainly, if he still has himself, a man of understanding has lost nothing.

When the city of Nola was sacked by the Barbarians, the local Bishop Paulinus lost everything and was thrown into prison; yet this was his prayer: 'Keep me O Lord from feeling this loss. Thou knowest that the Barbarians have so far touched nothing of mine.' Those riches which did enrich him and those good things which made him good were still intact.[16]

There you see what it means to choose treasures which no harm can corrupt and to hide them in a place which no one can enter, no one betray, save we ourselves. We should have wives, children, property and, above all, good health . . . if we can: but we should not become so attached to them that our happiness depends on them. We should set aside a room, just for ourselves, at the back of the shop, keeping it entirely free and establishing there our true liberty, our principal solitude and asylum. Within it our normal conversation should be of ourselves, with ourselves, so privy that no commerce or communication with the outside world should find a place there; there we should talk and laugh as though we had no wife, no children, no possessions, no followers, no menservants, so that when the occasion arises that we must lose them it should not be a new experience to do without them. We have a soul able to turn in on herself; she can keep herself company; she has the wherewithal to attack, to defend, to receive and to

16. St Augustine, *City of God*, I, x.

give. Let us not fear that in such a solitude as that we shall be crouching in painful idleness:

> *in solis sis tibi turba locis.*
> [in lonely places, be a crowd unto yourself.][17]

'Virtue,' says Antisthenes, 'contents herself, without regulations, words or actions.' Not even one in a thousand of our usual activities has anything to do with our self.

That man you can see over there, furiously beside himself, scrambling high up on the ruins of that battlement, the target of so many volleys from harquebuses; and that other man, all covered with scars, wan, pale with hunger, determined to burst rather than open the gate to him: do you think they are in it for themselves? It could well be for someone they have never seen, someone plunged meanwhile in idleness and delights, who takes no interest in what they are doing. And this man over here, rheumy, filthy and blear-eyed, whom you can see coming out of his work-room at midnight! Do you think he is looking in his books for ways to be better, happier, wiser? Not a bit. He will teach posterity how to scan a verse of Plautus and how to spell a Latin word, or else die in the attempt.

Is there anyone not willing to barter health, leisure and life itself against reputation and glory, the most useless, vain and counterfeit coinage in circulation? Our own deaths have never frightened us enough, so let us burden ourselves with fears for the deaths of our wives,

17. Tibullus, IV, xiii, 12 (adapted).

children and servants. Our own affairs have never caused us worry enough, so let us start cudgelling and tormenting our brains over those of our neighbours and of those whom we love.

> *Vah! quemquamne hominem in animum instituere, aut*
> *Parare, quod sit charius quam ipse est sibi?*
[Eh? Should a man prepare a settled place in his soul for something dearer than himself!][18]

It seems to me that solitude is more reasonable and right for those who, following the example of Thales, have devoted to the world their more active, vigorous years.

We have lived quite enough for others: let us live at least this tail-end of life for ourselves. Let us bring our thoughts and reflections back to ourselves and to our own well-being. Preparing securely for our own withdrawal is no light matter: it gives us enough trouble without introducing other concerns. Since God grants us leave to make things ready for our departure, let us prepare for it; let us pack up our bags and take leave of our company in good time; let us disentangle ourselves from those violent traps which pledge us to other things and which distance us from ourselves. We must unknot those bonds and, from this day forth, love this or that but marry nothing but ourselves. That is to say, let the rest be ours, but not so glued and joined to us that it cannot be pulled off without tearing away a piece of

18. Terence, *Adelphi*, I, i, 13–14.

ourselves, skin and all. The greatest thing in the world is to know how to live to yourself.

It is time to slip our knots with society now that we can contribute nothing to it. A man with nothing to lend should refrain from borrowing. Our powers are failing: let us draw them in and keep them within ourselves. Whoever can turn round the duties of love and fellowship and pour them into himself should do so. In that decline which makes a man a useless encumbrance importunate to others, let him avoid becoming an encumbrance, importunate and useless to himself. Let him pamper himself, cherish himself, but above all control himself, so respecting his reason and so fearing his conscience that he cannot stumble in their presence without shame: '*Rarum est enim ut satis se quisque vereatur.*' [It is rare for anybody to respect himself enough.][19] Socrates says that youth must get educated; grown men employ themselves in good actions; old men withdraw from affairs, both civil and military, living as they please without being bound to any definite duties.

There are complexions more suited than others to these maxims about retirement. Those who hold on to things slackly and weakly, and whose will and emotions are choosy, accepting neither slavery nor employment easily – and I am one of them, both by nature and by conviction – will bend to this counsel better than those busy active minds which welcome everything with open arms, which take on everything, get carried away about everything and which are always giving themselves,

19. Quintilian, X, 7.

offering themselves, putting themselves forward. When any good things happen to come to us from outside we should make use of them, so long as they remain pleasurable; we must not let them become our principal base, for they are no such thing: neither reason nor Nature will have them so. Why do we go against Nature's laws and make our happiness a slave in the power of others?

Yet to go and anticipate the injuries of Fortune, depriving ourselves of such good things as are still in our grasp, as several have done out of devotion and a few philosophers out of rational conviction, making slaves of themselves, sleeping rough, poking out their own eyes, chucking their wealth into rivers, going about looking for pain – the first to acquire blessedness in the next life because of torment in this one, the others to ensure against tumbling afresh by settling for the bottom rung – are actions of virtue taken to excess. Let tougher sterner natures make even their hiding-places glorious and exemplary.

> *tuta et parvula laudo,*
> *Cum res deficiunt, satis inter vilia fortis:*
> *Verum ubi quid melius contingit et unctius, idem*
> *Hos sapere, et solos aio bene vivere, quorum*
> *Conspicitur nitidis fundata pecunia villis.*

[When I lack money, I laud the possession of a few things which are sure; I show fortitude enough among paltry goods: but – still the same person – when anything better, more sumptuous, comes my way, then I say that only they are wise and live right well whose income is grounded in handsome acres.][20]

20. Horace, *Epistles*, I, xv, 42–6.

I have enough to do without going that far. When Fortune favours me, it is enough to prepare for her disfavour, picturing future ills in comfort, to the extent that my imagination can reach that far, just as we train ourselves in jousts and tournaments, counterfeiting war in the midst of peace. I do not reckon that Arcesilaus the philosopher had reformed his mind any the less because I know he used such gold and silver vessels as the state of his fortune allowed: for using them frankly and in moderation I hold him in greater esteem than if he had got rid of them.

I know how far our natural necessities can extend; and when I reflect that the indigent beggar at my door is often more merry and healthy than I am, I put myself firmly in his place and make an assay at giving my soul a slant like his. Then by running similarly through other examples, though I may think that death, poverty, contempt and sickness are dogging my heels, I can readily resolve not to be terrified by what a man of lesser estate than mine can accept with such patience. I cannot believe that a base intelligence can do more than a vigorous one or that reason cannot produce the same effects as habit. And since I realize how insecure these adventitious comforts are, my sovereign supplication, which I never fail to make to God, is that, even while I enjoy them fully, He may make me content with myself and with such goods as are born within me. I know healthy young men who travel with a mass of pills in their baggage to swallow during an attack of rheum, fearing it less since they know they have a remedy to hand. That is the way to do it, only more so: if you know yourself subject to some grave affliction, equip yourself with medicines to benumb and deaden the part concerned.

The occupation we must choose for a life like this one should be neither toilsome nor painful (otherwise we should have vainly proposed seeking such leisure). It depends on each man's individual taste. My taste is quite unsuited to managing my estates: those who do like it, should do it in moderation:

> *Conentur sibi res, non se submittere rebus.*
> [They should try to subordinate things to themselves, not themselves to things.][21]

Otherwise management, as Sallust puts it, is a servile task.[22] (Some aspects of it are more acceptable, such as an interest in gardening – which Xenophon attributes to Cyrus.)[23] A mean can be found between that base unworthy anxiety, full of tension and worry, seen in those who immerse themselves in it, and that profound extreme neglect one sees in others, who let everything go to rack and ruin:

> *Democriti pecus edit agellos*
> *Cultaque, dum peregre est animus sine corpore velox.*
> [Democritus left his herds to ravage fields and crops, while his speeding soul was wandering outside his body.][24]

21. Horace, *Epistles*, I, i, 19.     22. Sallust, *Catilinae coniuratio*, IV.
23. Cicero, *De Senectute*, XVI, 59.
24. Horace, *Epistles*, I, xii, 12–13.

But let us just listen to the advice about solitude which Pliny the Younger gave to his friend Cornelius Rufus: 'I counsel you in that ample and thriving retreat of yours, to hand the degrading and abject care of your estates over to those in your employ, and to devote yourself to the study of letters so as to derive from it something totally your own.'[25] By that, he means a good reputation, his humour being similar to Cicero's who said he wanted to use his withdrawal and his repose from the affairs of State to gain life everlasting through his writings!

> *Usque adeo ne*
> *Scire tuum nihil est, nisi te scire hoc sciat alter?*

[Does *knowing* mean nothing to you, unless somebody else knows that you know it?][26]

It seems logical that when you talk about withdrawing from the world you should be contemplating things outside it; they only half do that: they do indeed arrange their affairs for when they will no longer be in the world, yet the fruits of their project they claim to draw from the world they have left: a ridiculous contradiction.

The thought of those who seek solitude for devotion's sake, filling their minds with the certainty of God's promises for the life to come, is much more sane and appropriate. Their objective is God, infinite in goodness and power: the soul can find there matters to slake her desires in perfect freedom. Pains and afflictions are

25. Pliny the Younger, *Epistles*, I, i. no. 3.
26. Persius, *Satires*, I, xxiii.

profitable to them, being used to acquire eternal healing and joy; death is welcome as a passing over to that perfect state. The harshness of their Rule is smoothed by habit; their carnal appetites are rejected and lulled asleep by their denial – nothing maintains them but practising them and using them. Only this end, another life, blessedly immortal, genuinely merits our renunciation of the comforts and sweetnesses of this life of ours. Whoever can, in reality and constancy, set his soul ablaze with the fire of this lively faith and hope, builds in his solitude a life of choicest pleasures, beyond any other mode of life.

Neither the end, then, nor the means of Pliny's counsel satisfy me: we are always jumping from feverish fits into burning agues. Spending time with books has its painful side like everything else and is equally inimical to health, which must be our main concern; we must not let our edge be blunted by the pleasure we take in books: it is the same pleasure as destroys the manager of estates, the miser, the voluptuary and the man of ambition.

The wise men teach us well to save ourselves from our treacherous appetites and to distinguish true wholesome pleasures from pleasures diluted and crisscrossed by pain. Most pleasures, they say, tickle and embrace us only to throttle us, like those thieves whom the Egyptians called *Philistae*.[27] If a hangover came before we got drunk we would see that we never drank to excess: but pleasure, to deceive us, walks in front and hides her train. Books give pleasure: but if frequenting them eventually leads

27. Seneca, *Epist. moral.*, LI, 13; the *Philistae* (or *Philetai*) were assassins.

to loss of our finest accomplishments, joy and health, then give up your books. I am one who believes that their fruits cannot outweigh a loss such as that.

As men who have long felt weakened by illness in the end put themselves at the mercy of medicine and get that art to prescribe a definite diet never to be transgressed: so too a man who withdraws pained and disappointed with the common life must rule his life by a diet of reason, ordering it and arranging it with argument and forethought. He should have taken leave of toil and travail, no matter what face they present, and should flee from all kinds of passion which impede the tranquillity of his body and soul, and choose the way best suited to his humour.

> *Unusquisque sua noverit ire via.*
> [Let each man choose the road he should take.][28]

Whether we are running our home or studying or hunting or following any other sport, we should go to the very boundaries of pleasure but take good care not to be involved beyond the point where it begins to be mingled with pain. We should retain just enough occupations and pursuits to keep ourselves fit and to protect ourselves from the unpleasantness which comes in the train of that other extreme: slack and inert idleness.

There are branches of learning both sterile and prickly, most of them made for the throng: they may be left to those who serve society. Personally I only like pleasur-

---

28. Propertius, II, xxv, 38.

able easy books which tickle my interest, or those which console me and counsel me how to control my life and death.

> *Tacitum sylvas inter reptare salubres,*
> *Curantem quidquid dignum sapiente bonoque est.*

[Walking in silence through the healthy woods, pondering questions worthy of the wise and good.][29]

Wiser men with a strong and vigorous soul can forge for themselves a tranquillity which is wholly spiritual. Since my soul is commonplace, I must help sustain myself with the pleasures of the body – and since age has lately robbed me of those more pleasing to my fancy I am training and sharpening my appetite for those which are left, more suited to my later season. We must cling tooth and claw to the use of the pleasures of this life which the advancing years, one after another, rip from our grasp.

> *Carpamus dulcia; nostrum est*
> *Quod vivis: cinis et manes et fabula fies.*

[Let us pluck life's pleasures: it is up to us to live; you will soon be ashes, a ghost, something to tell tales about.][30]

As for glory – the end proposed by Pliny and Cicero – that is right outside my calculations. Ambition is the humour most contrary to seclusion. Glory and tranquillity cannot dwell in the same lodgings. As far as I can see, those authors have withdrawn only their arms and

29. Horace, *Epistles*, I, iv, 4–5.  30. Persius, *Satires*, V, 151–2.

legs from the throng: their souls, their thoughts, remain even more bound up with it.

> *Tun', vetule, auriculis alienis colligis escas?*
> [Now then, old chap, are you collecting bait to catch the ears of others?][31]

They step back only to make a better jump, and, with greater force, to make a lively charge through the troops of men.

Would you like to see how they fall just a tiny bit short of the target? Let us weigh against them the counsels of two philosophers – and from two different schools at that – one of them writing to his friend Idomeneus and the other to his friend Lucilius, to persuade them to give up the management of affairs of state and their great offices and to withdraw into solitude:[32]

'You have (they said) lived up to the present floating and tossing about; come away into the harbour and die. You have devoted your life to the light: devote what remains to obscurity. It is impossible to give up your pursuits if you do not give up their fruits. Renounce all concern for name and glory. There is the risk that the radiance of your former deeds may still cast too much light upon you and pursue you right into your lair. Among other gratifications give up the one which comes from other people's approval. As for your learned intelligence, do not worry about that: it will not lose its effect

31. Persius, *Satires*, I, 19–20.
32. The first is Epicurus. The second is Seneca. The following epistle is largely composed of borrowings from various epistles of Seneca.

if you yourself are improved by it. Remember the man who was asked why he toiled so hard at an art which few could ever know about: "For me a few are enough; one is enough; having none is enough." He spoke the truth. You and one companion are audience enough for each other; so are you for yourself. For you, let the crowd be one, and one be a crowd. It is a vile ambition in one's retreat to want to extract glory from one's idleness. We must do like the beasts and scuff out our tracks at the entrance to our lairs. You should no longer be concerned with what the world says of you but with what you say to yourself. Withdraw into yourself, but first prepare yourself to welcome yourself there. It would be madness to entrust yourself to yourself, if you did not know how to govern yourself. There are ways of failing in solitude as in society. Make yourself into a man in whose sight you would not care to walk awry; feel shame for yourself and respect for yourself, – *'observentur species honestae animo'* [let your mind dwell on examples of honour];[33] until you do, always imagine that you are with Cato, Phocion and Aristides, in whose sight the very madmen would hide their faults; make them recorders of your inmost thoughts, which, going astray, will be set right again out of reverence for them.

'The path they will keep you on is that of being contented with yourself, of borrowing all from yourself, of arresting and fixing your soul on thoughts contained within definite limits where she can find pleasure; then, having recognized those true benefits which we enjoy

33. Cicero, *Tusc. disput.*, II, xxii, 52.

the more the more we know them, content yourself with them, without any desire to extend your life or fame.'

That is the advice of a philosophy which is natural and true, not like that of those other two, all verbiage and show.

# On Books

I do not doubt that I often happen to talk of things which are treated better in the writings of master-craftsmen, and with more authenticity. What you have here is purely an assay of my natural, not at all of my acquired, abilities. Anyone who catches me out in ignorance does me no harm: I cannot vouch to other people for my reasonings: I can scarcely vouch for them to myself and am by no means satisfied with them. If anyone is looking for knowledge let him go where such fish are to be caught: there is nothing I lay claim to less. These are my own thoughts, by which I am striving to make known not matter but me. Perhaps I shall master that matter one day; or perhaps I did do so once when Fortune managed to bring me to places where light is thrown on it. But I no longer remember anything about that. I may be a man of fairly wide reading, but I retain nothing.

So I guarantee you nothing for certain, except my making known what point I have so far reached in my knowledge of it. Do not linger over the matter but over my fashioning of it. Where my borrowings are concerned, see whether I have been able to select something which improves my theme: I get others to say what I cannot put so well myself, sometimes because of the weakness of my language and sometimes because of the weakness of my intellect. I do not count my borrowings: I weigh them; if I had wanted them valued for their number I would have burdened myself with twice as many. They are all, except for very, very few, taken from names so famous and ancient that they seem to name themselves without help from me. In the case of those reasonings and original ideas which I transplant into my own soil and confound with my own, I sometimes deliberately omit to give the author's name so as to rein in the temerity of those hasty criticisms which leap to attack writings of every kind, especially recent writings by men still alive and in our vulgar tongue which allow anyone to talk about them and which seem to convict both their conception and design of being just as vulgar. I want them to flick Plutarch's nose in mistake for mine and to scald themselves by insulting the Seneca in me. I have to hide my weakness beneath those great reputations. I will love the man who can pluck out my feathers – I mean by the perspicacity of his judgement and by his sheer ability to distinguish the force and beauty of the topics. Myself, who am constantly unable to sort out my borrowings by my knowledge of where they came from, am quite able to measure my reach and to know that my own soil is in no wise capable of bringing forth some of the richer flowers that I find rooted there and which all the produce of my own growing could never match.

What I am obliged to answer for is for getting myself tangled up, or if there is any inanity or defect in my reasoning which I do not see or which I am incapable of seeing once it is pointed out to me. Faults can often escape our vigilance: sickness of judgement consists in not perceiving them when they are revealed to us. Knowledge and truth can lodge within us without judgement; judgement can do so without them: indeed, recognizing our ignorance is one of the surest and most beautiful witnesses to our judgement that I can find.

I have no sergeant-major to marshal my arguments other than Fortune. As my ravings present themselves, I pile them up; sometimes they all come crowding together: sometimes they drag along in single file. I want people to see my natural ordinary stride, however much it wanders off the path. I let myself go along as I find myself to be; anyway the matters treated here are not such that ignorance of them cannot be permitted nor talking of them casually or rashly. I would very much love to grasp things with a complete understanding but I cannot bring myself to pay the high cost of doing so. My design is to spend whatever life I have left gently and unlaboriously. I am not prepared to bash my brains for anything, not even for learning's sake however precious it may be. From books all I seek is to give myself pleasure by an honourable pastime: or if I do study, I seek only that branch of learning which deals with knowing myself and which teaches me how to live and die well:

*Has meus ad metas sudet oportet equus.*
[This is the winning-post towards which my sweating horse must run.][1]

If I come across difficult passages in my reading I never bite my nails over them: after making a charge or

1. Propertius, IV, i, 70.

two I let them be. If I settled down to them I would waste myself and my time, for my mind is made for the first jump. What I fail to see during my original charge I see even less when I stubborn it out.

I can do nothing without gaiety: persistence and too much intensity dazzle my judgement, making it sad and weary. My vision becomes confused and dissipated: I must tell it to withdraw and then make fresh glancing attacks, just as we are told to judge the sheen of scarlet-cloth by running our eyes over it several times, catching various glimpses of it, sudden, repeated and renewed.

If one book wearies me I take up another, applying myself to it only during those hours when I begin to be gripped by boredom at doing nothing. I do not have much to do with books by modern authors, since the Ancients seem to me to be more taut and ample; nor with books in Greek, since my judgement cannot do its job properly on the basis of a schoolboy, apprenticed understanding.

Among books affording plain delight, I judge that the *Decameron* of Boccaccio, Rabelais and the *Basia* of Johannes Secundus (if they are to be placed in this category) are worth spending time on. As for the *Amadis* and such like, they did not have enough authority to captivate me even in childhood. I will also add, boldly or rashly, that this aged heavy soul of mine can no longer be tickled by good old Ovid (let alone Ariosto): his flowing style and his invention, which once enraptured me, now hardly have the power of holding my attention.

I freely say what I think about all things – even about those which doubtless exceed my competence and which

I in no wise claim to be within my jurisdiction. When I express my opinions it is so as to reveal the measure of my sight not the measure of the thing. When I find that I have no taste for the *Axiochus* of Plato – a weak book, considering its author – my judgement does not trust itself: it is not so daft as to oppose the authority of so many other judgements, famous and ancient, which it holds as its professors and masters: rather is it happy to err with them. It blames itself, condemning itself either for stopping at the outer rind and for being unable to get right down to the bottom of things, or else for looking at the matter in some false light. My judgement is quite content merely to protect itself from confusion and unruliness: as for its weakness, it willingly acknowledges it and avows it. What it thinks it should do is to give a just interpretation of such phenomena as its power of conception presents it with: but they are feeble ones and imperfect. Most of Aesop's fables have several senses and several ways of being understood. Those who treat them as myths select some aspect which squares well with the fable; yet in most cases that is only the first surface facet of them: there are other facets, more vivid, more of their essence, more inward, to which they never manage to penetrate; that is what I do.

But to get on: it has always seemed to me that in poetry Virgil, Lucretius, Catullus and Horace rank highest by far – especially Virgil in his *Georgics*, which I reckon to be the most perfect achievement in poetry; by a comparison with it one can easily see that there are passages in the *Aeneid* to which Virgil, if he had been able, would have given a touch of the comb. And in the

*Aeneid* the fifth book seems to me the most perfect. I also love Lucan and like to be often in his company, not so much for his style as for his own worth and for the truth of his opinions and judgements. As for that good poet Terence – the grace and delight of the Latin tongue – I find him wonderful at vividly depicting the emotions of the soul and the modes of our behaviour; our own actions today constantly bring me back to him. However often I read him I always find some new grace and beauty in him.

Those who lived soon after Virgil's time complained that some put Lucretius on a par with him. My opinion is that such a comparison is indeed between unequals; yet I have quite a job confirming myself in that belief when I find myself enthralled by one of Lucretius' finer passages. If they were irritated by that comparison what would they say of the animal stupidity and barbarous insensitivity of those who now compare Ariosto with him? And what would Ariosto himself say?

> *O seclum insipiens et infacetum!*
> [O what a silly, tasteless age!][2]

I reckon that the Ancients had even more reason to complain of those who put Plautus on a par with Terence (who savours much more of the nobleman) than of those who did so for Lucretius and Virgil. It does much for Terence's reputation and superiority that the Father of Roman Eloquence has him – alone in his class – often

---

2. Catullus, XLIII, 8.

on his lips, and so too the verdict which the best judge among Roman poets gave of his fellow-poet.

It has often occurred to me that those of our contemporaries who undertake to write comedies (such as the Italians, who are quite good at it) use three or four plots from Terence or Plautus to make one of their own. In one single comedy they pile up five or six tales from Boccaccio. What makes them so burden themselves with matter is their lack of confidence in their ability to sustain themselves with their own graces: they need something solid to lean on; not having enough in themselves to captivate us they want the story to detain us. In the case of my author, Terence, it is quite the reverse: the perfections and beauties of the fashioning of his language make us lose our craving for his subject: everywhere it is his elegance and his graciousness which hold us; everywhere he is so delightful –

*liquidus puroque simillimus amni*
[flowing exactly like a pure fountain][3]

– and he so fills our souls to the brim with his graces that we forget those of his plot.

Considerations like these encourage me to go further: I note that the good poets of Antiquity avoided any striving to display not only such fantastic hyperboles as the Spaniards and the Petrarchists do but even those sweeter and more restrained acute phrases which adorn all works of poetry in the following centuries. Yet not

3. Horace, ibid., II, ii, 120.

one sound judge regrets that the Ancients lacked them nor fails to admire the incomparable even smoothness and the sustained sweetness and flourishing beauty of the epigrams of Catullus above the sharp goads with which Martial enlivens the tales of his. The reason for this is the same as I stated just now, and as Martial said of himself: *'Minus illi ingenio laborandum fuit, in cuius locum materia successerat.'* [He had less need to strive after originality, its place had been taken by his matter.][4] Those earlier poets achieve their effects without getting excited and goading themselves on; they find laughter everywhere: they do not have to go and tickle themselves! The later ones need extraneous help: the less spirit they have, the more body they need. They get up on their horses because they cannot stand on their own legs. It is the same with our dancing: those men of low estate who teach it are unable to copy the deportment and propriety of our nobility and so try to gain favour by their daring footwork and other strange acrobatics. And it is far easier for ladies to cut a figure in dances which require a variety of intricate bodily movements than in certain other stately dances in which they merely have to walk with a natural step and display their native bearing and their usual graces. Just as some excellent clowns whom I have seen are able to give us all the delight which can be drawn from their art while wearing their everyday clothes, whereas to put us in a laughing mood their apprentices and those who are less deeply learned in that art have to put flour on their faces, dress

4. Martial, *Epigrams*, VIII, dedication to the Emperor Domitian.

up in funny clothes and hide behind silly movements and grimaces.

Better than any other way this idea as I conceive it can be understood from a comparison between the *Aeneid* and the *Orlando furioso*. We can see the *Aeneid* winging aloft with a firm and soaring flight, always pursuing its goal: the *Orlando furioso* we see hopping and fluttering from tale to tale as from branch to branch, never trusting its wings except to cross a short distance, seeking to alight on every hedge lest its wind or strength should give out,

> *Excursusque breves tentat.*
> [Trying out its wings on little sorties.][5]

So much, then, for the authors who delight me most on that kind of subject.

As for my other category of books (that which mixes a little more usefulness with the delight[6] and from which I learn how to control my humours and my qualities), the authors whom I find most useful for that are Plutarch (since he has become a Frenchman) and Seneca. They both are strikingly suited to my humour in that the knowledge that I seek from them is treated in pieces not sewn together (and so do not require me to bind myself to some lengthy labour, of which I am quite incapable). Such are the *Moral Works* of Plutarch, as well as the *Epistles* of Seneca which are the most beautiful part of his writings and the most profitable. I do not need a

5. Virgil, *Georgics*, V, 194.     6. Horace, *Ars poetica*, 343.

great deal of preparation to get down to them and I can drop them whenever I like, for one part of them does not really lead to another. Those two authors are in agreement over most useful and true opinions; they were both fated to be born about the same period; both to be the tutors of Roman Emperors; both came from foreign lands and both were rich and powerful. Their teachings are some of the cream of philosophy and are presented in a simple and appropriate manner. Plutarch is more uniform and constant: Seneca is more diverse and comes in waves. Seneca stiffens and tenses himself, toiling to arm virtue against weakness, fear and vicious appetites; Plutarch seems to judge those vices to be less powerful and to refuse to condescend to hasten his step or to rely on a shield. Plutarch holds to Plato's opinions, which are gentle and well-suited to public life: Seneca's opinions are Stoic and Epicurean, farther from common practice but in my judgement more suited to the individual and firmer. It seems that Seneca bowed somewhat to the tyranny of the Emperors of his day, for I hold it for certain that his judgement was under duress when he condemned the cause of those great-souled murderers of Caesar; Plutarch is a free man from end to end. Seneca is full of pithy phrases and sallies; Plutarch is full of matter. Seneca enflames you and stirs you: Plutarch is more satisfying and repays you more. Plutarch leads us: Seneca drives us.

As for Cicero, the works of his which are most suitable to my projects are those which above all deal with moral philosophy. But to tell the truth boldly (for once we have crossed the boundaries of insolence there is no reining us in) his style of writing seems boring to me, and so do all similar styles. For his introductory passages, his definitions, his sub-divisions and his etymologies eat up most of his work; what living marrow there is in him is smothered by the tedium of his preparations. If I spend an hour reading him (which is a lot for me) and then recall what pith and substance I have got out of him, most of the time I find nothing but wind, for he has not yet got to the material which serves my purposes and to the reasoning which actually touches on the core of what I am interested in. For me, who am only seeking to become more wise not more learned or more eloquent, all those marshallings of Aristotelian logic are irrelevant; I want authors to begin with their conclusion: I know well enough what is meant by death or voluptuousness: let them not waste time dissecting them; from the outset I am looking for good solid reasons which teach me how to sustain their attacks. Neither grammatical subtleties nor ingenuity in weaving words or arguments help me in that. I want arguments which drive home their first attack right into the strongest point of doubt: Cicero's hover about the pot and languish. They are all right for the classroom, the pulpit or the Bar where we are free to doze off and find ourselves a quarter of an hour later still with time to pick up the thread of the argument. You have to talk like that to judges whom you want to win over whether you are right or wrong, or to school-boys and the common people to whom you have to say the lot and see what strikes home. I do not want authors to strive to gain my attention by crying *Oyez* fifty times like our heralds. The Romans in their religion used to cry *Hoc age!* [This do!], just as in our own we cry *Sursum corda* [Lift up your hearts]; for me they are so many wasted words. I leave home fully prepared: I need no sauce or appetizers: I can eat my meat quite raw; and instead of whetting my appetite with those preliminaries and preparations they deaden it for me and dull it.

Will the licence of our times excuse my audacious sacrilege in thinking that even Plato's *Dialogues* drag slowly along stifling his matter, and in lamenting the time spent on those long useless preparatory discussions by a man who had so many better things to say? My ignorance may be a better excuse, since I can see none of the beauty of his language.

In general I ask for books which use learning not those which trim it up.

My first two, as well as Pliny and their like, have no *Hoc age*: they want to deal with people who are already on the alert – or if they do have one it is an *Hoc age* of substance with its own separate body.

I also like reading Cicero's *Letters to Atticus*, not only because they contain much to teach us about the history and affairs of his time but, even more, so as to find out from them his private humours. For as I have said elsewhere I am uniquely curious about my authors' soul and native judgement. By what their writings display when they are paraded in the theatre of the world we can indeed judge their talents, but we cannot judge them as men nor their morals.

I have regretted hundreds of times that we have lost the book which Brutus wrote about virtue: it is a beautiful thing to learn the theory from those who thoroughly know the practice; yet seeing that the preacher and the preaching are two different things, I am just as happy to see Brutus in Plutarch as in a book of his own. I would rather have a true account of his chat with his private friends in his tent on the eve of a battle than the oration which he delivered next morning to his army, and what he did in his work-room and bedroom than what he did in the Forum or Senate.

As for Cicero, I share the common opinion that, erudition apart, there was little excellence in his soul. He was a good citizen, affable by nature as fat jolly men like him frequently are; but it is no lie to say that his share of weakness and ambitious vanity was very great. I cannot excuse him for reckoning his poetry worth publishing; it is no great crime to write bad verses but it was an error of judgement on his part not to have known how unworthy they were of the glory of his name.

As for his eloquence it is beyond compare; I believe no one will ever equal it. The younger Cicero, who resembled his father only in name, when in command of Asia found there were several men whom he did not know seated at his table: among others there was Caestius at the foot of it, where people often sneak in to enjoy the open hospitality of the great. Cicero asked one of his men who he was and was told his name; but, as a man whose thoughts were elsewhere and who kept forgetting the replies to his questions, he asked it him again two or three times. The servant, to avoid the bother of having to go on repeating the same thing and so as to enable Cicero to identify the man by something about him, replied, 'It is that man called Caestius who is said not to think much of your father's eloquence compared to his own.' Cicero, suddenly provoked by that, ordered his men to grab hold of that wretched Caestius and, in his presence, to give him a good flogging. A most discourteous host![7]

Even among those who reckoned that his eloquence was, all things considered, beyond compare, there were some who did not omit to draw attention to some defects in it; such as his friend the great Brutus who said it was an eloquence *'fractam et elumbem'* – 'broken and dislocated'.[8] Orators living near his own time criticized him for the persistent trouble he took to end his periods with lengthy cadences, and noted that he often used in them the words *'esse videatur'* [it would seem to be].

Personally I prefer cadences which conclude more abruptly, cut into iambics. He too can, very occasionally, mix his rhythms quite roughly: my own ears pointed this sentence out to me: *'Ego vero me minus diu senem esse mallem, quam esse senem, antequam essem.'* [I indeed hold being old less long better than being old before I am.][9]

The historians play right into my court. They are pleasant and delightful; and at the same time Man in general whom I seek to know appears in them more alive and more entire than in any other sort of writing, showing the true diversity of his inward qualities, both wholesale and retail, the variety of ways in which he is put together and the events which menace him.

Now the most appropriate historians for me are those

7. Marcus Annaeus Seneca, *Suasiorae*, VIII.
8. Tacitus, *Oratores*, XVIII.        9. Cicero, *De Senectute*, X, 32.

who write men's lives, since they linger more over motives than events, over what comes from inside more than what happens outside. That is why, of historians of every kind, Plutarch is the man for me.

I am deeply sorry that we do not have Diogenes Laertiuses by the dozen, or that he himself did not spread himself more widely or more wisely, for I consider the lives and fortunes of the great teachers of mankind no less carefully than their ideas and doctrines.

In this genre – the study of history – we must without distinction leaf our way through all kinds of authors, ancient and modern, in pidgin and in French, so as to learn about the *matter* which they treat in their divergent ways. But Caesar seems to me to deserve special study, not only to learn historical facts but on his own account, since his perfection excels that of all others, even including Sallust.

I certainly read Caesar with rather more reverence and awe than is usual for the works of men, at times considering the man himself through his deeds and the miracle of his greatness, at others the purity and the inimitable polish of his language which not only surpassed that of all other historians, as Cicero said, but perhaps that of Cicero himself. There is such a lack of bias in his judgement when he talks of his enemies that the only thing you can reproach him with, apart from the deceptive colours under which he seeks to hide his bad cause and the filth of his pernicious ambition, is that he talks of himself too sparingly. For so many great things cannot have been done by him without he himself contributing more to them than he includes in his books.

I like either very simple historians or else outstanding ones. The simple ones, who have nothing of their own to contribute, merely bringing to their task care and diligence in collecting everything which comes to their attention and chronicling everything in good faith without choice or selection, leave our judgement intact for the discerning of the truth. Among others there is for example that good man Froissart who strides with such frank sincerity through his enterprise that when he has made an error he is never afraid to admit it and to correct it at whatever point he has reached when told about it; and he relates all the various rumours which were current and the differing reports that were made to him. Here is the very stuff of history, naked and unshaped: each man can draw such profit from it as his understanding allows.

The truly outstanding historians are capable of choosing what is worth knowing; they can select which of two reports is the more likely; from the endowments and humours of princes they can draw conclusions about their intentions and attribute appropriate words to them. Such historians are right to assume the authority of controlling what we accept by what they do: but that certainly belongs to very few.

Those who lie in between (as most historians do) spoil everything for us: they want to chew things over for us; they give themselves the right to make judgements and consequently bend history to their own ideas: for once our judgement leans to one side we cannot stop ourselves twisting and distorting the narration to that bias. They take on the task of choosing what is worth knowing, often hiding from us some speech or private action which would have taught us much more; they leave out things they find incredible because they do not understand them, and doubtless leave out others because they do not know how to put them into good Latin or French. Let them make a display of their rhetoric and their arguments if they dare to; let them judge as they like: but let them leave us the means of making our own judgements after them; let them not deprave by their abridgements nor arrange by their selection anything of material substance, but rather let them pass it all on to us purely and wholly, in all its dimensions.

As often as not, and especially in our own times, historiographers are appointed from among quite commonplace people, simply on account of their knowing how to write well, as though we wanted to learn grammar! They are right, having been paid to do that and having nothing but chatter to sell, to worry mainly about that aspect. And so with many a fine phrase they spin a web of rumours gathered at the crossroads of our cities.

The only good histories are those written by men who were actually in charge of affairs or who played some part in that charge, or who at least were fortunate enough to have been in charge of others of a similar kind. Such were virtually all the Greek and Roman historians. For, with several eye-witnesses having written on the same subject (as happened in those days when greatness and learning were commonly found together), if an error were made it must have been wonderfully slight, or concern some incident itself open to great doubt.

What can we hope from a doctor who writes about war, or a schoolboy writing about the designs of kings?

To realize how scrupulous the Romans were over this, we need only one example: Asinius Pollio found even in Caesar's histories some mistakes into which he had fallen because he had not been able to look with his own eyes at every part of his army and had believed individual men who had reported to him things which were often inadequately verified, or else because he had not been carefully enough informed by his commanders-delegate of their conduct of affairs during his absence.[10]

We can see from that example what a delicate thing our quest for truth is when we cannot even rely on the commander's knowledge of a battle he has fought nor on the soldiers' accounts of what went on round them unless, as in a judicial inquiry, we confront witnesses and accept objections to alleged proofs of the finer points of every occurrence. Truly, the knowledge we have of our own affairs is much slacker. But that has been adequately treated by Bodin, and in conformity with my own ideas.[11]

To help my defective and treacherous memory a little – and it is so extremely bad that I have more than once happened to pick up again, thinking it new and unknown to me, a book which I had carefully read several years earlier and scribbled all over with my notes – I have for some time now adopted the practice of adding at the end of each book (I mean of each book which I intend

10. Suetonius, *Life of Caesar*, LVI.
11. Jean Bodin, *Methodus ad facilem historiarum cognitionem*, Paris, 1566.

to read only once) the date when I finished reading it and the general judgement I drew from it, in order to show me again at least the general idea and impression I had conceived of its author when reading it. I would like to transcribe here some of those annotations.

Here is what I put about ten years ago on my Guicciardini (for no matter what language is spoken by my books, I speak to them in my own): 'He is an industrious writer of history, from whom in my judgement we can learn the truth about the affairs of his time more accurately than from any other; moreover he played a part in most of them, holding an honoured position. There is no sign that he ever disguised anything through hatred, favour or vanity; that is vouched for by the unfettered judgements he makes of the great, especially of those by whom he had been promoted to serve in responsible positions, such as Pope Clement VII. As for the quality in which he seems to want most to excel, namely his digressions and reflections, some are excellent and enriched by beautiful sketches; but he enjoyed them too much: he did not want to leave anything out, yet his subject was a full and ample one – infinite almost – and so he can become sloppy and somewhat redolent of academic chatter. I have also been struck by the following: that among all his judgements on minds and actions, among so many motives and intentions, he attributes not one of them to virtue, religious scruple or conscience, as if those qualities had been entirely snuffed out in our world; and among all those deeds, no matter how beautiful they might seem in themselves, he attributes their cause to some evil opportunity or gain. It is impossible to conceive that among the innumerable actions on which he makes a judgement there were not at least some produced by means of reason. No corruption can have infected everyone so totally that there was not some man or other who escaped the contagion. That leads me to fear that his own taste was somewhat corrupted: perhaps he happened to base his estimates of others on himself.'

This is what I have on my Philippe de Commines: 'You will find the language here smooth and delightful, of a natural simplicity; the narration pure, with the good faith of the author manifestly shining through it; himself free from vanity when talking of himself, and of favour and of envy when talking of others, together with a fine zeal for truth rather than any unusual acuteness; and from end to end, authority and weight showing him to be a man of good extraction and brought up to great affairs.'

And on the *Memoirs* of Monsieur Du Bellay, the following:

'It is always a pleasure to see things written about by those who had assayed how to manage them, but there is no denying that in these two noblemen there is clearly revealed a great decline from that shining frankness and freedom in writing found in older authors of their rank such as the Seigneur de Joinville (the close friend of Saint Louis), Eginhard (the Chancellor of Charlemagne) and more recently Philippe de Commines. This is not history so much as pleading the case of King Francis against the Emperor Charles V. I am unwilling to believe that they altered any of the major facts, but they make it their job to distort the judgement of events to our advantage, often quite unreasonably, and to pass over anything touchy in the life of their master: witness the fall from grace of the Seigneur de Montmorency and the Seigneur de Brion, which is simply omitted: indeed the very name of Madame d'Estampes is not to be found in them! Secret deeds can be hushed up, but to keep silent about things which everyone knows about, especially things which led to public actions of such consequence, is a defect which cannot be pardoned. In short if you take my advice you should look elsewhere for a full account of King Francis and the events of his time; what can be profitable are the particulars given of the battles and military engagements when these noblemen were present; a few private words and deeds of a few princes of their time; and the transactions and negotiations conducted by the Seigneur de Langey which are chock full of things worth knowing and of uncommon reflections.'

# On the Power of the Imagination

'*Fortis imaginatio generat casum*' [A powerful imagination generates the event], as the scholars say. I am one of those by whom the powerful blows of the imagination are felt most strongly. Everyone is hit by it, but some are bowled over. It cuts a deep impression into me: my skill consists in avoiding it not resisting it. I would rather live among people who are healthy and cheerful: the sight of another man's suffering produces physical suffering in me, and my own sensitivity has often misappropriated the feelings of a third party. A persistent cougher tickles my lungs and my throat.

The sick whom I am duty-bound to visit I visit more unwillingly than those with whom I feel less concerned and less involved. When I contemplate an illness I seize upon it and lodge it within myself: I do not find it strange that imagination should bring fevers and death to those who let it act freely and who give it encouragement.

In his own time Simon Thomas was a great doctor. I remember that I happened to meet him one day at the home of a rich old consumptive; he told his patient when discussing ways to cure him that one means was to provide occasions for me to enjoy his company: he could then fix his eyes on the freshness of my countenance and his thoughts on the overflowing cheerfulness and vigour of my young manhood; by filling all his senses with the flower of my youth his condition might improve. He forgot to add that mine might get worse.

Gallus Vibius so tensed his soul to understand the essence and impulsions of insanity that he toppled his own judgement from its seat and was never able to restore it again: he could boast that he was made a fool by his own wisdom.

Some there are who forestall the hand of their executioners; one man was on the scaffold, being unblindfolded so that his pardon could be read to him, when he fell down dead, the blow being struck by his imagination alone. When imaginary thoughts trouble us we break into sweats, start trembling, grow pale or flush crimson; we lie struck supine on our feather-beds and feel our bodies agitated by such emotions; some even die from them. And boiling youth grows so hot in its armour-plate that it consummates its sexual desires while fast asleep in a dream –

*Ut quasi transactis sæpe omnibus rebus profundant*
*Fluminis ingentes fluctus, vestemque cruentent.*
[So that, as though they had actually completed the act, they pour forth floods of semen and pollute their garments.][1]


It is no new thing for a man to wake up with cuckold's horns which he never had when he went to bed, but it is worth remembering what happened to Cyppus, a king in Italy: he had been very excited by a bullfight one day and his dreams that night had filled his head full of bulls'

1. Lucretius, IV, 1035–6.

horns: thereupon horns grew on his forehead by the sheer power of his imagination.[2]

Nature had denied the power of speech to the son of Croesus: passion gave it to him; Antiochus fell into a fever from the beauty of Stratonice, which was too vigorously imprinted on his soul; Pliny says that, on the very day of the wedding, he saw Lucius Cossitius change from woman to man; Pontanus and others tell of similar metamorphoses which have happened in Italy in recent centuries. And, since both Iphis' own desires and her mother's were so vehement,

> *Vota puer solvit, quae foemina voverat Iphis.*
> [Iphis fulfilled as a boy vows made as a girl.][3]

I was travelling through Vitry-le-François when I was able to see a man to whom the Bishop of Soissons had given the name of Germain at his confirmation: until the age of twenty-two he had been known by sight to all the townsfolk as a girl called Marie. He was then an old man with a full beard; he remained unmarried. He said that he had been straining to jump when his male organs suddenly appeared. (The girls there still have a song in which they warn each other not to take great strides lest they become boys, 'like Marie Germain'.) It is not surprising that this sort of occurrence happens frequently. For if the imagination does have any power in such matters, in girls it dwells so constantly and so

2. Pliny, XI, xlv.
3. Ovid, *Metamorphoses*, IX, 795ff.

forcefully on sex that it can (in order to avoid the necessity of so frequently recurring to the same thoughts and harsh yearnings) more easily make that male organ into a part of their bodies.

The scars of King Dagobert and of Saint Francis are attributed by some to the power of their imagination: and they say that by it bodies are sometimes transported from their places; Celsus gives an account of a priest whose soul was enraptured in such an ecstasy that for a considerable period his body remained breathless and senseless.[4] Saint Augustine gives the name of another priest who only needed to hear lamentations and plaintive cries to fall into a swoon, being carried so vigorously outside himself that, until he came back to life again, in vain would you shake him about, shout at him, pinch him or sear his flesh: the priest said he heard their voices, but as though coming from afar; he was also aware of the bruising and branding. That this was no stubborn concealing of his sense-impressions is shown by his being, during this time, without pulse or breath.[5]

It is likely that the credit given to miracles, visions, enchantments and such extraordinary events chiefly derives from the power of the imagination acting mainly on the more impressionable souls of the common people. Their capacity to believe has been so powerfully ravished that they think they see what they do not see. I am moreover of the opinion that those ridiculous attacks of magic impotence by which our society believes itself to

4. H. C. Agrippa, *De occulta philosophia*, I, lxiv.
5. St Augustine, *City of God*, XIV, xxiv.

be so beset that we talk of nothing else can readily be thought of as resulting from the impress of fear or apprehension. I know this from the experience of a man whom I can vouch for as though he were myself: there is not the slightest suspicion of sexual inadequacy in his case nor of magic spells; but he heard one of his comrades tell how an extraordinary impotency fell upon him just when he could least afford it; then, on a similar occasion, the horror of this account struck his own imagination so brutally that he too incurred a similar fate; from then on he was subject to relapses, the ignoble memory of his misadventure taunting him and tyrannizing over him. He found that this madness he could cure by another kind of madness: he admitted beforehand that he was subject to this infirmity and spoke openly about it, so relieving the tensions within his soul; by bearing the malady as something to be expected, his sense of constriction grew less and weighed less heavily upon him; then (his thoughts being unencumbered and relaxed) when an occasion arose to its liking, his body, finding itself in good trim for first sounding itself out, seizing itself and taking itself by surprise with its partner in the know, clean cured itself of that condition. Except for genuine impotence, never again are you incapable if you are capable of doing it once.

This misfortune is to be feared only in adventures where our souls are immoderately tense with desire and respect; especially when the opportunity is pressing and unforeseen, there is no means of recovering from this confusion. I know one man who found it useful to bring to it a body on the point of being satisfied elsewhere, in order to quieten the ardour of this frenzy and who, growing older, finds himself less impotent for being less potent.

Yet another found it helpful when a friend assured him that he was furnished with a counter-battery of enchantments certain to preserve him. I had better tell how that happened.

A highly placed Count with whom I was intimate was marrying a most beautiful lady who had long been courted by a guest present at the festivities; those who loved him were worried about him – especially one of his relations, an old lady who was presiding over the marriage (which was being held in her house): she feared there might be sorcery about and told me of it. I begged her to put her trust in me. I happened to have in my strong-boxes a certain little flat piece of gold on which were engraved celestial symbols, protecting against sunstroke and relieving headaches when correctly applied to the cranial suture; it was sewn on to a ribbon to be tied under the chin to keep it in place – a piece of lunacy akin to the one we are talking of. This peculiar present had been given me by Jacques Peletier: I decided to get some good out of it. I told the Count that he might well incur the same misfortune as others and that there were those who would willingly see that he did so: but he should go to the marriage-bed confidently since I would do him a friendly turn, not failing in his moment of need to perform a miracle which lay within my power, provided that he promised me on his honour to keep it most faithfully secret, simply giving me a sign if things had gone badly when we rushed in with the festive supper. Both his soul and his ears had received such a battering that, because of his troubled imagination, he had indeed been incapable of an erection: so he gave me the sign. He was then to get up (I had told him) under pretence of chasing us out, playfully seize the nightshirt I was holding (we were much the same size) and wear it until he had followed my prescription – which was as follows: as soon as we had left the room he was to withdraw to pass water: he was then to say certain prayers three times and make certain gestures: each time he was to tie round himself the ribbon I had put into his hand and carefully lay the attached medallion over his kidneys, with the figure in a specified position. Having done so, he should draw the ribbon tight so that it could not come undone: then he was to go back and confidently get on with the job, not forgetting to throw my night-shirt over his bed in such a way as to cover them both.

It is such monkeyings-about which mainly produce results: our thoughts cannot free themselves from the convictions that such strange actions must derive from some secret lore. Their weight and respect come from their inanity. In short the figures on my talisman proved to have more to do with Venus than with the Sun, more potent in action than as a prophylactic.

I was led to do this deed (which is so foreign to my nature) by a rash and troubled humour. I am opposed to all feigned and subtle actions; I hate sleight of hand not only in games but even when it serves a purpose. The way is vicious even if the deed is not.

Amasis, a King of Egypt, wed Laodice, a very beautiful Grecian maiden. He was a pleasant companion in every other way, but he was incapable of lying with her; he threatened to kill her, thinking there had been some witchcraft. Appropriately enough where mental apprehensions are concerned, she deflected his attention towards invocations: having made his vows and prayers to Venus, he found that very night, after his sacrificial oblations, that he had been divinely restored.[6]

Women are wrong to greet us with those affected provocative appearances of unwillingness which snuff out our ardour just as they kindle it. The daughter-in-law of Pythagoras used to say that a woman who lies with a man should doff her modesty with her kirtle and don it again with her shift.[7] The heart of an attacker is easily dismayed when disturbed by calls to arms which are many and diverse; it is a bad start, once imagination makes a man suffer this shame (which she only does in those first encounters, since they are tempestuous and eager: it is in the first encounter that one most fears a defeat); this occurrence then puts him into a feverish moodiness which persists when subsequent opportunities arise.

Married folk have time at their disposal: if they are not ready they should not try to rush things. Rather than fall into perpetual wretchedness by being struck with despair at a first rejection, it is better to fail to make it properly on the marriage-couch, full as it is of feverish agitation, and to wait for an opportune moment, more private and less challenging. Before possessing his wife, a man who suffers a rejection should make gentle assays

6. Herodotus, II, clxxxi.
7. Cf. Plutarch (tr. Amyot), *Preceptes de mariage*, VIII.

and overtures with various little sallies; he should not stubbornly persist in proving himself inadequate once and for all. Those who know that their member is naturally obedient should merely take care to out-trick their mental apprehensions.

We are right to note the licence and disobedience of this member which thrusts itself forward so inopportunely when we do not want it to, and which so inopportunely lets us down when we most need it; it imperiously contests for authority with our will: it stubbornly and proudly refuses all our incitements, both mental and manual. Yet if this member were arraigned for rebelliousness, found guilty because of it and then retained me to plead its cause, I would doubtless cast suspicion on our other members for having deliberately brought a trumped-up charge, plotting to arm everybody against it and maliciously accusing it alone of a defect common to them all. I ask you to reflect whether there is one single part of our body which does not often refuse to function when we want it to, yet does so when we want it not to. Our members have emotions proper to themselves which arouse them or quieten them down without leave from us. How often do compelling facial movements bear witness to thoughts which we were keeping secret, so betraying us to those who are with us? The same causes which animate that member animate – without our knowledge – the heart, the lungs and the pulse: the sight of some pleasant object can imperceptibly spread right through us the flame of a feverish desire. Is it only the veins and muscles of that particular member which rise or fall without the consent of our will or even of our very thoughts? We do not command our hair to stand on end with fear nor our flesh to quiver with desire. Our hands often go where we do not tell them; our tongues can fail, our voices congeal, when *they* want to. Even when we have nothing for the pot and would fain order our hunger and thirst not to do so, they never fail to stir up those members which are subject to them, just as that other appetite does: it also deserts us, inopportunely, whenever it wants to. That sphincter which serves to discharge our stomachs has dilations and contractions proper to itself, independent of our wishes or even opposed to them; so do those members which are destined to discharge the kidneys.

To show the limitless authority of our wills, Saint Augustine cites the example of a man who could make his behind produce farts whenever he would: Vives in his glosses goes one better with a contemporary example of a man who could arrange to fart in tune with verses recited to him; but that does not prove the pure obedience of that member, since it is normally most indiscreet and disorderly.[8] In addition I know one Behind so stormy and churlish that it has obliged its master to fart forth wind constantly and unremittingly for forty years and is thus bringing him to his death.

Yet against our very will (on behalf of whose rights we have drawn up this bill of accusation) can be brought a prima-facie charge of sedition and rebellion because of its own unruliness and disobedience. Does it always wish what we want it to? Does it not often wish what we

8. St Augustine, *City of God*, XIV, xxiv.

forbid it to – and that to our evident prejudice? Is it any more subject to the determinations of our reason? Finally, on behalf of my noble client, may it please the Court to consider that, in this matter, my client's case is indissolubly conjoined to a consort from whom he cannot be separated. Yet the suit is addressed to my client alone, employing arguments and making charges which (granted the properties of the Parties) can in no wise be brought against the aforesaid consort. By which it can be seen the manifest animosity and legal impropriety of the accusers. The contrary notwithstanding, Nature registers a protest against the barristers' accusations and the judges' sentences, and will meanwhile proceed as usual, as one who acted rightly when she endowed the aforesaid member with its own peculiar privilege to be the author of the only immortal achievement known to mortals. For which reason, generation is held by Socrates to be god-like, and Love, that desire for immortality, to be himself a *Daemon* and immortal.

One man, perhaps by the power of his imagination, leaves in France the very scrofula which his fellow then takes back into Spain. That is why it is customary to insist in such matters that the soul lend her consent. Why do doctors first work on the confidence of their patient with so many fake promises of a cure if not to allow the action of the imagination to make up for the trickery of their potions? They know that one of the masters of their craft told them in writing that there are men for whom it is enough merely to look at a medicine for it to prove effective.

That sudden whim of mine all came back to me

because of a tale told me by one of my late father's servants who was an apothecary. He was a simple man – a Swiss (a people little given to vanity and lying). He had had a long acquaintance with a sickly merchant in Toulouse who suffered from the stone; he had frequent need of enemas and made his doctors prescribe him various kinds, depending on the symptoms of his illness. When the enemas were brought in, none of the usual formalities were omitted: he often used to finger them to see if they were too hot. There he was, lying down and turned on his side; all the usual preliminaries were gone through . . . except that no clyster was injected! After this ceremony the apothecary withdrew; the patient was treated as though he had taken the clyster and the result was the same as for those who had. If the doctor found that the treatment did not prove effective he gave him two or three other enemas – all of the same kind! Now my informant swears that the sick man's wife (in order to cut down expenses, since he paid for these clysters as though he had really had them) assayed simply injecting warm water; that proved to have no effect: the trickery was therefore discovered but he was obliged to return to the first kind.

There was a woman who believed she had swallowed a pin in her bread; she yelled and screamed as though she felt an insufferable pain in her throat where she thought she could feel it stuck; but since there was no swelling nor external symptoms, one clever fellow concluded that it was all imagination and opinion occasioned by a crust that had jabbed her on the way down; he made her vomit and secretly tossed a bent pin into what she had brought up. That woman believed that she had vomited it out and immediately felt relieved of the pain.

I know of a squire who had entertained a goodly company in his hall and then, four or five days later, boasted as a joke (for there was no truth in it) that he had made them eat cat pie; one of the young ladies in the party was struck with such horror at this that she collapsed with a serious stomach disorder and a fever: it was impossible to save her.

Even the very beasts are subject to the power of the imagination just as we are. Witness dogs, which grieve to death when they lose their masters. We can also see dogs yapping and twitching in their dreams, while horses whinny and struggle about.

But all this can be attributed to the close stitching of mind to body, each communicating its fortunes to the other. It is quite a different matter that the imagination should sometimes act not merely upon its own body but on someone else's. One body can inflict an illness on a neighbouring one (as can be seen in the case of the plague, the pox and conjunctivitis which are passed on from person to person):

> *Dum spectant oculi læsos, læduntur et ipsi:*
> *Multaque corporibus transitione nocent.*

[Looking at sore eyes can make your own eyes sore; and many ills are spread by bodily infection.][9]

---

9. Ovid, *De remedio amoris*, 615–16.

Similarly when the imagination is vehemently shaken it sends forth darts which may strike an outside object. In antiquity it was held that when certain Scythian women were animated by anger against anybody they could kill him simply by looking at him. Tortoises and ostriches hatch out their eggs by sight alone – a sign that they emit certain occult influences.[10] And as for witches, they are said to have eyes which can strike and harm:

> *Nescio quis teneros oculus mihi fascinat agnos*
> [An eye, I know not whose, has bewitched my tender lambs.][11]

For me magicians provide poor authority. All the same we know from experience that mothers can transmit to the bodies of children in their womb marks connected with their thoughts – witness that woman who gave birth to a blackamoor. And near Pisa there was presented to the Emperor Charles, King of Bohemia, a girl all bristly and hairy whom her mother claimed to have conceived like this because of a portrait of John the Baptist hanging above her bed. It is the same with animals: witness Jacob's sheep and those partridges and hares which are turned white by the snow in the mountains. In my own place recently a cat was seen watching a bird perched high up a tree; they stared fixedly at each other for some little time when the bird tumbled dead between the paws of the cat: either its own imagination had poisoned it or else it had been drawn by the cat's force of attraction. Those who are fond of hawking know

10. Pliny, VII, ii, and IX, x.    11. Virgil, *Eclogue*, III, 103.

the tale of the falconer who fixed his gaze purposefully on a kite as it flew and bet he could bring it down by the sheer power of his sight. And he did.

Or so they say: for when I borrow *exempla* I commit them to the consciences of those I took them from. The discursive reflexions are my own and depend on rational proof not on experience: everyone can add his own examples; if anyone has none of his own he should not stop believing that such *exempla* exist, given the number and variety of occurrences. If my *exempla* do not fit, supply your own for me. In the study I am making of our manners and motives, fabulous testimonies – provided they remain possible – can do service as well as true ones. Whether it happened or not, to Peter or John, in Rome or in Paris, it still remains within the compass of what human beings are capable of; it tells me something useful about that. I can see this and profit by it equally in semblance as in reality. There are often different versions of a story: I make use of the one which is rarest and most memorable. There are some authors whose aim is to relate what happened: mine (if I could manage it) would be to relate what can happen. When details are lacking Schoolmen are rightly permitted to posit probabilities. I do not: where this is concerned I excel all historical fidelity in my devoted scrupulousness. Whenever my *exempla* concern what I have heard, what I have said or what I have done, I have not dared to allow myself to change even the most useless or trivial of circumstances. I do not know about my science, but not one jot has been consciously falsified.

While on this topic I often wonder how Theologians

or philosophers and their like, with their exquisite consciences and their exacting wisdom, can properly write history. How can they pledge their own trustworthiness on the trustworthiness of ordinary people? How can they vouch for the thoughts of people they have never known and offer their own conjectures as sound coinage? They would refuse to bear sworn witness in Court about complex actions which actually occurred in their presence; there is no man so intimate with them that they would undertake to give a full account of all his thoughts.

I think it less risky to write about the past than the present, since the author has only to account for borrowed truth. Some have invited me to write about contemporary events, reckoning that I see them with eyes less vitiated by passion than others do and that I have a closer view than they, since Fortune has given me access to the various leaders of the contending parties. What they do not say is that I would not inflict such pain upon myself for all the fame of Sallust (being as I am the sworn enemy of binding obligations, continuous toil and perseverance), nor that nothing is so foreign to my mode of writing than extended narration. I have to break off so often from shortness of wind that neither the structure of my works nor their development is worth anything at all; and I have a more-than-childish ignorance of the words and phrases used in the most ordinary affairs. That is why I have undertaken to talk about only what I know how to talk about, fitting the subject-matter to my capacities. Were I to choose a subject where I had to be led, my capacities might prove inadequate to it. They do not say either that, since my freedom is so very free, I could have published judgements which even I would reasonably and readily hold to be unlawful and deserving of punishment. Of his own achievement Plutarch would be the first to admit that if his *exempla* are wholly and entirely true that is the work of his sources: his own work consisted in making them useful to posterity, presenting them with a splendour which lightens our path towards virtue.

An ancient account is not like a doctor's prescription, every item in it being tother or which.

# On Sadness

I am among those who are most free from this emotion; I neither like it nor think well of it, even though the world, by common consent, has decided to honour it with special favour. Wisdom is decked out in it; so are Virtue and Conscience – a daft and monstrous adornment. More reasonably it is not sadness but wickedness that the Italians have baptised *tristezza* [sadness], for it is a quality which is ever harmful, ever mad. The Stoics forbid this emotion to their sages as being base and cowardly.

But a story is told about Psammenitus, a King of Egypt. When he was defeated and captured by Cambises the King of Persia he showed no emotion as he saw his daughter walk across in front of him, dressed as a servant and sent to draw water. All his friends were about him, weeping and lamenting: he remained quiet, his eyes fixed on the ground. Soon afterwards he saw his son led away to execution; he kept the same countenance. But when he saw one of his household friends brought in among the captives, he began to beat his head and show grief.[1]

You can compare that with what we recently saw happen to one of our princes.[2] He was at Trent: first he heard the news of the death of his very special elder

1. Erasmus, *Apophthegmata; varie mixta: Diversum Graecorum*, IX (*Opera*, 1703–6, Vol. IV, col. 304EF).
2. Charles de Guise, Cardinal de Lorraine (at the Council of Trent).

brother, the support and pride of his whole family; then came the death of his younger brother, their second hope. He bore both these blows with exemplary fortitude; yet, when a few days later one of his men happened to die, he let himself be carried away by this event; he abandoned his resolute calm and gave himself over to grief and sorrow – so much so that some argued that only this last shock had touched him to the quick. The truth is that he was already brimful of sadness, so the least extra burden broke down the barriers of his endurance.

We could, I suggest, put the same interpretation on the story of Psammenitus, except that the account goes on to tell us that Cambises asked him why he had remained unmoved by the fate of his son and daughter yet showed such emotion at the death of his friend. 'Only the last of these misfortunes can be expressed by tears', he replied; 'the first two are way beyond any means of expression.'

That may explain the solution adopted by a painter in antiquity.[3] He had to portray the grief shown on the faces of the people who were present when Iphigenia was sacrificed, giving each of them the degree of sorrow appropriate to his feelings of involvement in the death of that fair and innocent young woman. By the time he came to portray the father of Iphigenia he had exhausted all the resources of his art, so he painted him with his face veiled over, as though no countenance could display a grief so intense.

That is why the poets feign that when Niobe lost

3. Timanthes (Cicero, *De Oratore*, XXII; Quintillian, II, xiii, 12).

seven sons and then seven daughters she was overcome by such bereavements and was finally turned into a rock:

> *Diriguisse malis.*
> [Petrified by such misfortunes.][4]

By this they expressed that sad, deaf, speechless stupor which seizes us when we are overwhelmed by tragedies beyond endurance.

The force of extreme sadness inevitably stuns the whole of our soul, impeding her freedom of action. It happens to us when we are suddenly struck with alarm by some really bad news: we are enraptured, seized, paralysed in all our movements in such a way that, afterwards, when the soul lets herself go with tears and lamentations, she seems to have struggled loose, disentangled herself and become free to range about as she wishes:

> *Et via vix tandem voic laxata dolore est.*
> [And then, at length, his grief can just force open a channel for his voice.][5]

In the war which King Ferdinand waged near Buda against the widow of King John of Hungary, there was a German officer called Raïsciac. As he saw men bringing back the body of a soldier slung across a horse, he joined in the general mourning for the man who had shown exceptional bravery in the clash of battle. Like the others

4. Ovid, *Metamorphoses*, VI, 304.    5. Virgil, *Aeneid*, XI, 151.

he was curious to know who the man was. When they took off the armour he recognized his son. Amid all the public tears he alone stood dry-eyed, saying nothing, his gaze fixed on his son until the violent strain of that sadness froze his vital spirits and, just as he was, toppled him dead to the ground.[6]

> *Chi puo dir com' egli arde e in picciol fuoco* –
[He who can describe how his heart is ablaze is burning on a small pyre][7] –

that is what lovers say when they want to express an unbearable passion.

> *misero quod omnes*
> *Eripit sensus mihi. Nam simul te,*
> *Lesbia, aspexi, nihil est super mi*
> *Quod loquar amens.*

> *Lingua sed torpet, tenuis sub artus*
> *Flamma dimanat, sonitu suopte*
> *Tinniunt aures, gemina teguntur*
> *Lumina nocte.*

[How pitiable I am. Love snatches my senses from me. As soon as I see you, Lesbia, I can say nothing to you; I am out of my mind; my tongue sticks in my mouth; a fiery flame courses through my limbs; my ears are ringing and darkness covers both my eyes.][8]

6. Paolo Giovio, *Historia sui temporis*, 1550, XXXIX.
7. Petrarch, Sonnet 137.     8. Catullus, LI, 5.

We cannot display our grief or our convictions during the living searing heat of the attack; the soul is then burdened by deep thought and the body is cast down, languishing for love. That is the source of the occasional impotence which sometimes comes so unseasonably upon men when making love, and of that chill produced, in the very lap of their delight by excessive ardour. For pleasures to be tasted and then digested they must remain moderate:

> *Curae leves loquuntur, ingentes stupent.*
> [Light cares can talk: huge ones are struck dumb.][9]

We can be equally stunned when surprised by joy unhoped for:

> *Ut me conspexit venientem, et Troïa circum*
> *Arma amens vidit, magnis exterrita monstris,*
> *Diriguit visu in medio, calor ossa reliquit,*
> *Labitur, et longo vix tandem tempore fatur.*

[As soon as she noticed me coming and saw the arms of Troy all about her, she went out of her mind. As though terrified by some dreadful portents her gaze became fixed upon them, the heat drained from her body; she fell to the ground and for a long time uttered not a word.][10]

There was a Roman woman who was surprised by joy on seeing her son return from the rout at Cannae

---

9. For pleasures . . . Seneca (the dramatist), *Hippolitus*, II, iii, 607.
10. Virgil, *Aeneid*, III, 306.

and fell down dead; Sophocles and Dionysius the Tyrant died of happiness; Talva died in Corsica upon reading the news of the honours conferred on him by the Senate. Apart from these it is claimed that in our own century Pope Leo X entered into such an excess of joy upon being told of the capture of Milan (his desire for which had been extreme) that he took fever and died.

And there is an even more noteworthy witness to human weakness: the Ancients recorded that Diodorus the Dialectician 'fell in the field', overcome by an extreme sense of shame at being unable to refute arguments put to him in public in the presence of his followers.

Violent emotions like these have little hold on me. By nature my sense of feeling has a hard skin, which I daily toughen and thicken by arguments.

# On Constancy

Resolution and constancy do not lay down as a law that we may not protect ourselves, as far as it lies in our power to do so, from the ills and misfortunes which threaten us, nor consequently that we should not fear that they may surprise us. On the contrary, all honourable means of protecting oneself from evils are not only licit: they are laudable. The role played by constancy consists chiefly in patiently bearing misfortunes for which there is no remedy. Likewise there are no evasive movements of the body and no defensive actions with any weapons in our hands which we judge wrong if they serve to protect us from the blows raining down on us.

Many highly warlike nations included flight as one of their main tactical resources: when they turned their backs that was more risky to the enemy than when they showed their faces. The Turks still retain this to some extent.

In Plato Socrates mocked Laches for defining fortitude as 'standing firm in line in the face of the enemy'. 'What,' he said, 'would it be cowardice to defeat them by giving ground?' And he cited Homer who praised Aeneas for knowing when to flee. And once Laches had corrected himself and allowed that the Scythians did use that method as do cavalrymen in general, he then went on to cite the example of those foot-soldiers of Sparta, a nation trained above all to stand their ground: during the battle of Plataea they found that they could not penetrate the Persian phalanx and so decided to disengage and fall back in order that it should be thought that they were in full flight; that would lead to the breaking up of the Persians' dense formation which would fall apart as it pursued them. By which means they obtained the victory.[1]

While on the subject of the Scythians, it is said that after Darius had set out to subjugate them, he sent many reproaches to their king when he saw him always withdrawing and avoiding battle. To this Indathyrsez (for that was the king's name) replied that he was not afraid of him nor of any man alive, but that this was the practice of his people, since they possessed no arable lands, no towns and no houses to defend for fear that an enemy might make use of them: but if Darius really was yearning to sink his teeth into a battle, then let him try to get near to their ancient burial grounds: he would find somebody to talk to there![2]

Nevertheless once a man's post is the target of cannon-fire (as the chances of war often require it to be) it is unbecoming for him to waver before the threatening cannon-balls, all the more so since we hold that they have such speed and such impetus that you cannot take evasive action. There are many cases of soldiers at least providing their comrades with a good laugh by shielding behind their arms or ducking their heads.

Yet in the expedition which the Emperor Charles V

1. Plato, *Laches*, 190B–191D.    2. Herodotus, *Hist.*, IV, cxxvii.

led against us in Provence, when the Marquis de Guast went to reconnoitre the city of Arles and suddenly appeared from behind a windmill under cover of which he had made his advance, he was spotted by the Seigneur de Bonneval and the Lord Seneschal d'Agenois who were strolling along the top of the amphitheatre. They pointed him out to the Seigneur de Villier, Master of the Ordnance, who aimed a culverin so accurately that if the Marquis had not seen the match applied to the fuse and jumped aside it was thought he would have been struck in the body.[3] Similarly a few years before, when Lorenzo de' Medici, the Duke of Urbino and the father of our Queen Mother, was laying siege to Mondolfo (a fortress in Italy in the territory they call the Vicariate) he saw the fire applied to a cannon which was pointing right at him and ducked; luckily for him, for otherwise the shot, which only grazed the top of his head, would have certainly struck him in the chest.[4]

To tell the truth I do not believe that such movements arise from reflexion: for in so sudden a matter how can you judge whether the aim is high or low? It is far easier to believe that fortune looked favourably on their fear but that another time they might have jumped into the path of the shot not out of it.

Personally I cannot stop myself from trembling if the shattering sound of a harquebus suddenly strikes my ear in a place where I could not have expected it; I have seen that happen to more valorous men than I am. Not even

3. The invasion was in 1536. Cf. Du Bellay, *Mémoires*, VII, p. 129.

4. Francesco Guicciardini, *Historia d'Italia*, XIII, ii.

the Stoics claim that their sage can resist visual stimuli or ideas when they first come upon him; they concede that it is, rather, part of man's natural condition that he should react to a loud noise in the heavens or to the collapse of a building by growing tense and even pale. So too for all other emotions, provided that his thoughts remain sound and secure, that the seat of his reason suffer no impediment or change of any sort, and that he in no wise give his assent to his fright or pain. As for anyone who is not a sage, the first part applies to him but not the second. For in his case the impress of the emotions does not remain on the surface but penetrates through to the seat of his reason, infecting and corrupting it: he judges by his emotions and acts in conformity with them.

The state of the Stoic sage is fully and elegantly seen in the following:

*Mens immota manet, lachrimae volvuntur inanes.*
[His mind remains unmoved: empty tears do flow.]

The Aristotelian sage is not exempt from the emotions: he moderates them.[5]

5. All here from St Augustine, *City of God*, IX, iv.

# On Fear

*Obstupui, steteruntque comae, et vox faucibus haesit.*
[I stood dumb with fear; my hair stood on end and my voice
stuck in my throat.][1]

I am not much of a 'natural philosopher' – that is the
term they use; I have hardly any idea of the mechanisms
by which fear operates in us; but it is a very odd emotion
all the same; doctors say that there is no emotion
which more readily ravishes our judgement from its
proper seat. I myself have seen many men truly driven
out of their minds by fear, and it is certain that, while
the fit lasts, fear engenders even in the most staid of men
a terrifying confusion.

I leave aside simple folk, for whom fear sometimes
conjures up visions of their great-grandsires rising out
of their graves still wrapped in their shrouds, or else
of chimeras, werewolves or goblins; but even among
soldiers, where fear ought to be able to find very little
room, how many times have I seen it change a flock of
sheep into a squadron of knights in armour; reeds or
bulrushes into men-at-arms and lancers; our friends, into
enemies; a white cross into a red one.

When Monsieur de Bourbon captured Rome, a

---

1. Virgil, *Aeneid*, II, 774.

standard-bearer who was on guard at the Burgo San Pietro was seized by such terror at the first alarm that he leapt through a gap in the ruins and rushed out of the town straight for the enemy still holding his banner; he thought he was running into the town, but at the very last minute he just managed to see the troops of Monsieur de Bourbon drawing up their ranks ready to resist him (it was thought that the townsfolk were making a sortie); he realized what he was doing and headed back through the very same gap out of which he had just made a three-hundred-yards' dash into the battlefield.

But the standard-bearer of Captain Juille was not so lucky when Saint-Pol was taken from us by Count de Bures and the Seigneur de Reu; for fear had made him so distraught that he dashed out of the town, banner and all, through a gun-slit and was cut to pieces by the attacking soldiers. There was another memorable case during the same siege, when fear so strongly seized the heart of a certain nobleman, freezing it and strangling it, that he dropped down dead in the breach without even being wounded.[2]

Such fear can sometimes take hold of a great crowd. In one of the engagements between Germanicus and the Allemani two large troops of soldiers took fright and fled opposite ways, one fleeing to the place which the other had just fled from.[3]

Sometimes fear as in the first two examples puts wings on our heels; at others it hobbles us and nails our feet to the ground, as happened to the Emperor Theophilus in

2. Du Bellay, *Mémoires*, VIII, 255.    3. Tacitus, *Hist.*, I, lxiii.

the battle which he lost against the Agarenes; we read that he was so enraptured and so beside himself with fear, that he could not even make up his mind to run away: *'adeo pavor etiam auxilia formidat'* [so much does fear dread even help][4] Eventually Manuel, one of the foremost commanders of his army, shook him and pulled him roughly about as though rousing him from a profound sleep, saying, 'If you will not follow me I will kill you; the loss of your life matters less than the loss of the Empire if you are taken prisoner.'

Fear reveals her greatest power when she drives us to perform in her own service those very deeds of valour of which she robbed our duty and our honour. In the first pitched battle which the Romans lost to Hannibal during the consulship of Sempronius, an army of ten thousand foot-soldiers took fright, but seeing no other way to make their cowardly escape they fought their way through the thick of the enemy, driving right through them with incredible energy, slaughtering a large number of Carthaginians but paying the same price for a shameful flight as they should have done for a glorious victory.[5]

It is fear that I am most afraid of. In harshness it surpasses all other mischances. What emotion could ever be more powerful or more appropriate than that felt by the friends of Pompey who were aboard a ship with him and witnessed that horrible massacre of his forces? Yet even that emotion was stifled by their fear of the

4. Quintus Curtius, III, ii. The general account is from Joannes Zonaras, *Historia*, III.
5. Livy, *Annal.*, XXI, lvi.

Egyptian sails as they began to draw nearer; it was noticed that his friends had no time for anything but urging the sailors to strive to save them by rowing harder; but after they touched land at Tyre their fear left them and they were free to turn their thoughts to the losses they had just suffered and to give rein to those tears and lamentations which that stronger emotion of fear had kept in abeyance.

> *Tum pavor sapientiam omnem mihi ex animo expectorat.*
> [Then fear banishes all wisdom from my heart.][6]

Men who have suffered a good mauling in a military engagement, all wounded and bloody as they are, can be brought back to the attack the following day; but men who have tasted real fear cannot be brought even to look at the enemy again. People with a pressing fear of losing their property or of being driven into exile or enslaved also lose all desire to eat, drink or sleep, whereas those who are actually impoverished, banished or enslaved often enjoy life as much as anyone else. And many people, unable to withstand the stabbing pains of fear, have hanged themselves, drowned themselves or jumped to their deaths, showing us that fear is even more importunate and unbearable than death.

The Greeks acknowledged another species of fear over and above that fear caused when our reason is distraught; it comes, they say, from some celestial impulsion, with-

6. Cicero, *Tusc. disput.*, III, xxvii, 66. (The event figures in Shakespeare's *Antony and Cleopatra*.) Then ibid., IV, viii, 19, citing Ennius.

72

out any apparent cause.[7] Whole peoples have been seized by it as well as whole armies. Just such a fear brought wondrous desolation to Carthage: nothing was heard but shouts and terrified voices; people were seen dashing out of their houses as if the alarm had been sounded; they began attacking, wounding and killing each other, as though they took each other for enemies come to occupy their city. All was disorder and tumult until they had calmed the anger of their gods with prayer and sacrifice.

Such outbursts are called 'Panic terrors'.[8]

7. Diodorus Siculus, XV, vii.
8. Cf. Erasmus, *Adages*, III, VIII, III, *Panicus casus*; also *Apophthegmata*, V; *Epaminondas*, I.

# How Our Mind Tangles Itself Up

It is a pleasant thought to imagine a mind exactly poised between two parallel desires, for it would indubitably never reach a decision, since making a choice implies that there is an inequality of value; if anyone were to place us between a bottle and a ham when we had an equal appetite for drink and for food there would certainly be no remedy but to die of thirst and of hunger!

In order to provide against this difficulty the Stoics, when you ask them how our souls manage to choose between two things which are indifferent and how we come to take one coin rather than another from a large number of crowns when they are all alike and there is no reason which can sway our preference, reply that this motion in our souls is extraordinary and not subject to rules, coming into us from some outside impulse, incidental and fortuitous.

It seems to me that we could say that nothing ever presents itself to us in which there is not some difference, however slight: either to sight or to touch there is always an additional something which attracts us even though we may not perceive it.

Similarly if anyone would postulate a cord, equally strong throughout its length, it is impossible, quite impossible, that it should break. For where would you want it to start to fray? And it is not in nature for it all to break at once.

Then if anyone were to follow that up with those geometrical propositions which demonstrate by convincing demonstrations that the container is greater than the thing contained and that the centre is as great as the circumference, and which can find two lines which ever approach each other but can never meet, and then with the philosopher's stone and the squaring of the circle, where reason and practice are so opposed, he would perhaps draw from them arguments to support the bold saying of Pliny: '*Solum certum nihil esse certi, et homine nihil miserius aut superbius.*' [There is nothing certain except that nothing is certain, and nothing more wretched than Man nor more arrogant.][1]

1. A saying of Pliny's (*Hist. nat.*, II, vii) which Montaigne inscribed in his library.

# On Conscience

During our civil wars I was travelling one day with my brother the Sieur de la Brousse when we met a gentleman of good appearance who was on the other side from us; I did not know anything about that since he feigned otherwise. The worst of these wars is that the cards are so mixed up, with your enemy indistinguishable from you by any clear indication of language or deportment, being brought up under the same laws, manners and climate, that it is not easy to avoid confusion and disorder. That made me fear that I myself would come upon our own troops in a place where I was not known, be obliged to state my name and wait for the worst. That did happen to me on another occasion: for, from just such a mishap, I lost men and horses. Among others, they killed one of my pages, pitifully: an Italian of good family whom I was carefully training; in him was extinguished a young life, beautiful and full of great promise.

But that man of mine was so madly afraid! I noticed that he nearly died every time we met any horsemen or passed through towns loyal to the King; I finally guessed that his alarm arose from his conscience. It seemed to that wretched man that you could read right into the very secret thoughts of his mind through his mask and the crosses on his greatcoat. So wondrous is the power of conscience! It makes us betray, accuse and fight against

ourselves. In default of an outside testimony it leads us
to witness against ourselves:

> *Occultum quatiens animo tortore flagellum.*
> [Lashing us with invisible whips, our soul torments us.][1]

The following story is on the lips of children: a Paeon-
ian called Bessus was rebuked for having deliberately
destroyed a nest of swallows, killing them all. He said he
was right to do so: those little birds kept falsely accusing
him of having murdered his father! Until then this act of
parricide had been hidden and unknown; but the aveng-
ing Furies of his conscience made him who was to pay
the penalty reveal the crime.[2]

Hesiod corrects that saying of Plato's, that the punishment follows hard upon the sin. He says it is born at the
same instant, with the sin itself; to expect punishment is
to suffer it: to merit it is to expect it. Wickedness forges
torments for itself,

> *Malum consilium consultori pessimum,*
> [Who counsels evil, suffers evil most,][3]

just as the wasp harms others when it stings but especially
itself, for it loses sting and strength for ever:

1. Juvenal, *Satires*, XIII, 195 (adapted).
2. Plutarch (tr. Amyot), *Pourquoy la justice divine differe la punition des malefices*, 261 E C (a major borrowing).
3. Erasmus, *Adages*, I, II, XIV, *Malum consilium*.

*Vitasque in vulnere ponunt.*
[In that wound they lay down their lives.]⁴

The Spanish blister-fly secretes an antidote to its poison, by some mutual antipathy within nature. So too, just when we take pleasure in vice, there is born in our conscience an opposite displeasure, which tortures us, sleeping and waking, with many painful thoughts.

*Quippe ubi se multi, per somnia sæpe loquentes,*
*Aut morbo delirantes, procraxe ferantur,*
*Et celata diu in medium peccata dedisse.*
[Many indeed, often talking in their sleep or delirious in illness, have proclaimed, it is said, and betrayed long-hidden sins.]⁵

Apollodorus dreamed that he saw himself being flayed by the Scythians then boiled in a pot while his heart kept muttering, 'I am the cause of all these ills.' No hiding-place awaits the wicked, said Epicurus, for they can never be certain of hiding there while their conscience gives them away.⁶

*Prima est hæc ultio, quod se*
*Judice nemo nocens absolvitur.*
[This is the principal vengeance: no guilty man is absolved: he is his own judge.]⁷

4. Virgil, *Georgics*, IV, 238.     5. Lucretius, V, 1157–9.
6. Plutarch (tr. Amyot), *Pourquoy la justice divine diffère*, 262 D-E; Seneca, *Epist. moral.*, XCVII, 13.
7. Juvenal, *Satires*, XIII, 2–3.

Conscience can fill us with fear, but she can also fill us with assurance and confidence. And I can say that I have walked more firmly through some dangers by reflecting on the secret knowledge I had of my own will and the innocence of my designs.

> *Conscia mens ut cuique sua est, ita concipit intra*
> *Pectora pro facto spemque metumque suo.*

[A mind conscious of what we have done conceives within our breast either hope or fear, according to our deeds.][8]

There are hundreds of examples: it will suffice to cite three of them about the same great man.

When Scipio was arraigned one day before the Roman people on a grave indictment, instead of defending himself and flattering his judges he said: 'Your wishing to judge, on a capital charge, a man through whom you have authority to judge the Roman world, becomes you well!'

Another time his only reply to the accusations made against him by a Tribune of the People was not to plead his cause but to say: 'Come, fellow citizens! Let us go and give thanks to the gods for the victory they gave me over the Carthaginians on just such a day as this!' Then as he started to walk towards the temple all the assembled people could be seen following after him – even his prosecutor.

Again when Petilius, under the instigation of Cato, demanded that Scipio account for the monies that had

---

8. Ovid, *Fasti*, I, 485–6.

passed through his hands in the province of Antioch, Scipio came to the Senate for this purpose, took his account-book from under his toga and declared that it contained the truth about his receipts and expenditure; but when he was told to produce it as evidence he refused to do so, saying that he had no wish to act so shamefully towards himself; in the presence of the Senate he tore it up with his own hands. I do not believe that a soul with seared scars could have counterfeited such assurance. He had, says Livy, a mind too great by nature, a mind too elevated by Fortune, even to know how to be a criminal or to condescend to the baseness of defending his innocence.[9]

Torture is a dangerous innovation; it would appear that it is an assay not of the truth but of a man's endurance. The man who can endure it hides the truth: so does he who cannot. For why should pain make me confess what is true rather than force me to say what is not true? And on the contrary if a man who has not done what he is accused of is able to support such torment, why should a man who has done it be unable to support it, when so beautiful a reward as life itself is offered him?

I think that this innovation is founded on the importance of the power of conscience. It would seem that in the case of the guilty man it would weaken him and assist the torture in making him confess his fault, whereas it strengthens the innocent man against the torture. But to speak the truth, it is a method full of danger and

9. Plutarch (tr. Amyot), *Comment on se peut louer soy-mesme*, 139 F; Aulus Gellius, *Attic Nights*, IV, xviii; Livy, *Annales*, XXXVIII.

uncertainty. What would you *not* say, what would you *not* do, to avoid such grievous pain?

> *Etiam innocentes cogit mentiri dolor.*
> [Pain compels even the innocent to lie.]

This results in a man whom the judge has put to the torture lest he die innocent being condemned to die both innocent and tortured.[10] Thousands upon thousands have falsely confessed to capital charges. Among them, after considering the details of the trial which Alexander made him face and the way he was tortured, I place Philotas.[11]

All the same it is, so they say, the least bad method that human frailty has been able to discover. Very inhumanely, however, and very ineffectually in my opinion. Many peoples less barbarous in this respect than the Greeks and the Romans who call them the Barbarians reckon it horrifying and cruel to torture and smash a man of whose crime you are still in doubt. That ignorant doubt is yours: what has it to do with him? You are the unjust one, are you not? who do worse than kill a man so as not to kill him without due cause! You can prove that by seeing how frequently a man prefers to die for no reason at all rather than to pass through such a questioning which is more painful than the death-penalty itself and which by its harshness often anticipates that penalty by carrying it out.

---

10. St Augustine, *City of God*, XIX, vi.
11. Quintus Curtius, VI ff.

I do not know where I heard this from, but it exactly represents the conscience of our own Justice: a village woman accused a soldier before his commanding general – a great man for justice – of having wrenched from her little children such sops as she had left to feed them with, the army having laid waste all the surrounding villages. As for proof, there was none. That general first summoned the woman to think carefully what she was saying, especially since she would be guilty of perjury if she were lying; she persisted, so he had the soldier's belly slit open in order to throw the light of truth on to the fact. The woman was found to be right. An investigatory condemnation!

# On Anger

Plutarch is amazing in every respect but especially where he makes judgements on men's actions. In his parallel lives of Lycurgus and Numa we can see the beauty of what he says when treating of our great stupidity in abandoning children to the responsibility and control of their fathers. The majority of our polities, as Aristotle says, are like the Cyclops, abandoning the guidance of the women and children to each individual man according to his mad and injudicious ideas: hardly any, except the polities of Sparta and of Crete, have entrusted the education of children to their laws.[1] Anyone can see that all things within a State depend upon the way it educates and brings up its children. Yet quite injudiciously that is left to the mercy of the parents, no matter how mad or wicked they may be.

How many times have I been tempted, among other things, to make a dramatic intervention so as to avenge some little boys whom I saw being bruised, knocked about and flayed alive by some frenzied father or mother beside themselves with anger. You can see fire and rage flashing from their eyes –

1. Aristotle, *Nicomachaean Ethics*, X, ix, 1180a (with, for Crete, I, xiii, 1102a).

> *rabie iecur incendente, feruntur*
> *Præcipites, ut saxa iugis abrupta, quibus mons*
> *Subtrahitur, clivoque latus pendente recedit*

[they are carried away by burning wrath, like boulders wrenched free from the cliff crashing down the precipitous slope]

(according to Hippocrates the most dangerous of distempers are those which contort the face)[2] – as with shrill wounding voices, they scream at children who are often barely weaned. Children are crippled and knocked stupid by such batterings: yet our judicial system takes no note of it, as though it were not the very limbs of our State which are thus being put out of joint and maimed.

> *Gratum est quod patriæ civem populoque dedisti,*
> *Si facis ut patriæ sit idoneus, utilis agris,*
> *Utilis et bellorum et pacis rebus agendis.*

[It is good to have given a citizen to the people and the State – provided that you make him fit for his country, good at farming, good in war and peace.][3]

No passion disturbs the soundness of our judgement as anger does. No one would hesitate to punish with death a judge who was led to condemn his man as a criminal out of anger: then why is it any more permissible for fathers and schoolmasters to punish and flog children in anger? That is no longer correction, it is vengeance.

2. Juvenal, VI, 647–9; Hippocrates, in Plutarch (tr. Amyot), *Comment il fault refrener la colere* 579–H and, later, 60 E.
3. Juvenal, XIV, 70–3.

For a child punishment is a medicine: would we tolerate a doctor who was animated by wrath against his patient? We ourselves, if we would act properly, should never lay a hand on our servants as long as our anger lasts. While our pulse is beating and we can feel the emotion, let us put off the encounter: things will really and truly look different to us once we have cooled off a bit and quietened down. Until then passion is in command, passion does all the talking, not us. Faults seen through anger are like objects seen through a mist: they appear larger. If a man is hungry, then let him eat food: but he should never hunger and thirst for anger if he intends to chastise.

And then punishments applied after being judiciously weighed are more acceptable and more useful to the sufferer. Otherwise he does not think that he has been justly condemned by a man shaking with anger and fury; he cites in his own justification the inflamed face of the schoolmaster, his unaccustomed swearing, his mental disturbance and his precipitate haste.

> *Ora tument ira, nigrescunt sanguine venæ,*
> *Lumina Gorgoneo sævius igne micant.*

[His face swells with anger, the blood darkens in his veins and his eyes flash with fire more savage than a Gorgon's.][4]

Suetonius relates that Lucius Saturninus, after being condemned by Caesar, was helped in winning his case before the People (to whom he had appealed) above all by the bitter animus that Caesar brought to his verdict.

---

4. Ovid, *De arte amandi*, III, 503–4.

Saying is one thing: doing is another; we must consider the preaching apart and the preacher apart. Those who in our own time have made an assay at shaking the truth taught in our Church by citing the vices of her ministers have given themselves an easy game. Her testimonies are drawn from elsewhere. That way of arguing is stupid: it would throw everything into confusion. A man of good morals may hold false opinions: a wicked man can preach the truth – yes, even truths he does not believe. It is most certainly harmonious and beautiful when saying and doing go together; I have no wish to deny that saying has more authority and efficacity when followed by doing – as Eudamidas remarked on hearing a philosopher discoursing about war: 'Beautiful words: but the man who spoke them cannot be believed since his ears are not used to the sound of the trumpet.' And when Cleomenes heard a professor of rhetoric declaiming about valour he burst out laughing; the professor was scandalized but Cleomenes replied: 'I would do the same if it were a swallow speaking: now if it were an eagle, I would willingly listen.'[5]

It seems to me that I can perceive from the writings of the Ancients that the man who says what he really thinks drives it home in a livelier way than he who only pretends. Listen to Cicero talking about the love of liberty: then listen to Brutus! The very writings declare that Brutus was the man to purchase liberty at the cost of his life. Let Cicero, the father of eloquence, treat the theme of contempt for death; let Seneca treat it too:

5. Plutarch (tr. Amyot), *Dicts notables des Lacedaemoniens*, 216–18.

Cicero drags it out lifelessly and you can feel that he wants to make you resolute about something for which he himself has no resolution at all. He cannot put heart into you: he has none to give. But Seneca rouses you and inflames you.

I never read an author, especially one treating of virtue and duty, without curiously inquiring what sort of man he was. The Ephors of Sparta, on seeing a dissolute man giving useful advice in a speech before the people, ordered him to stop and requested a man of honour to sponsor the new idea and to speak for it.[6]

The writings of Plutarch if you savour them well adequately reveal him – and I believe that I know Plutarch, penetrating even into his soul. Yet I could wish that we had some personal memoirs. If I have let myself go in this digression it is because of the gratitude I feel towards Aulus Gellius for having bequeathed to us in his writings the following account of his manners which touches again on my subject: anger.

One of Plutarch's slaves, a bad, wicked man whose ears had however drunk in a few lectures in philosophy, had been stripped for some crime by order of Plutarch; at first, while he was being flogged, he snarled about its not being right and that he had not done anything wrong; but in the end he started to shout abuse at his master in good earnest, accusing him of not really being a philosopher as he boasted, since he had often heard him say that it was ugly to get angry and had even written a

6. Plutarch (tr. Amyot), *Comment il fault ouir*, 26G. Then, Aulus Gellius, I, xxvi.

book on the subject; the fact that he was now immersed in anger and having him cruelly flogged completely gave the lie to his writings. To which Plutarch, quite without heat and completely calm, replied: 'What makes you think, you ruffian, that I am angry at this time? Does my face, my voice, my colouring or my speech bear any witness to my being excited? I do not think my eyes are wild, my face distorted nor my voice terrifying. Is my face inflamed? Am I foaming at the mouth? Do words escape me which I will later regret? Am I all a-tremble? Am I shaking with wrath? Those, I can tell you, are the true symptoms of anger.' Then turning towards the man who was doing the flogging he said, 'Carry on with your job, while this man and I are having a discussion.'

That is the account in Aulus Gellius.

On returning from a war in which he had served as Captain-General, Archytas of Tarentum found in his house every sign of mismanagement and his lands lying fallow through the neglect of his steward. He summoned him before him and said, 'Go. If I were not so angry I would give you a good going over.' So too Plato: when he was inflamed against one of his slaves he handed him over to Speucippus for punishment, apologizing for not laying hands on him himself since he was angry. Charillus, a Spartan, said to a helot who was behaving most insolently and audaciously toward him: 'By the gods! If I were not so angry I would have you put to death at once.'[7]

7. Plutarch (tr. Amyot), *Comment il fault nourrir les enfans*, 6D–E; *Dicts notables des anciens Roys*, 198 F–G.

Anger is a passion which delights in itself and fawns on itself. How often, if we are all worked up for some wrong reason and then offered some good defence or excuse, we are vexed against truth and innocence itself! I can recall a marvellous example of this from Antiquity. Piso, a great man in every other way, noted for his virtue, was moved to anger against one of his soldiers. Because that soldier had returned alone after foraging and could give no account of where he had left his comrade, Piso was convinced that he had murdered him and at once condemned him to death. When he was already on the gallows, along comes the lost comrade! At this the whole army was overjoyed and, after many a hug and embrace between the two men, the executioner brought both of them into the presence of Piso; all those who were there were expecting that Piso himself would be delighted. Quite the contrary: for, through embarrassment and vexation, his fury, which was still very powerful, suddenly redoubled and, by a quibble which his passion promptly furnished him with, he found three men guilty because one had just been found innocent, and had all three of them executed: the first soldier because he was already sentenced to death; the second, the one who had gone missing, because he had caused the death of his comrade; the hangman for failing to obey orders.[8]

Those who have had to deal with obstinate women may have made an assay of the raging madness that they are thrown into when you confront their agitated minds

8. Seneca, *De ira*, I, xvi.

with silence and coldness and do not condescend to feed their bad temper. Celius the orator was of a marvellously choleric nature. There was, dining in his company, a man of mild and gentle manners who, so as not to provoke him, decided to approve of everything he said and always to agree with him; but Celius could not tolerate that his evil temper should thus pass unfed and exclaimed: 'For the gods' sake challenge something that I say, so that there can be two of us!'[9] Similarly women get angry only to make us angry in turn, imitating the laws of love. Phocion, when a man kept interrupting what he was saying with bitter insults, simply stopped talking, giving him enough time to exhaust his choler; when that was over, without mentioning the disturbance, he took up his speech just where he had left off. No retort goads a man more sharply than disdain such as that.

Of the most choleric man in France (and it is always a defect, though pardonable in a fighting man since in the exercise of that profession there are certainly situations where it cannot be dispensed with) I often say that he is in fact the most long-suffering man I know in restraining his choler. It shakes him with such violence and frenzy –

> *magno veluti cum flamma sonore*
> *Virgea suggeritur costis undantis aheni,*
> *Exultantque æstu latices; furit intus aquaï*
> *Fumidus atque alte spumis exuberat amnis;*
> *Nec jam se capit unda; volat vapor ater ad auras*

9. Seneca, *De ira*, III, viii; then, Plutarch, *Instruction pour ceulx qui manient affaires d'Estat*, 169 B.

[as when, beneath a brazen cauldron, the fire roars noisily into flame and licks its sides, the water boils with the heat and, madly foaming in its prison, breaks over the edge and can contain itself no longer, sending black fumes off into the air]

– that, to moderate it, he has to keep himself under cruel restraint.[10] Personally I know of no passion of mine for which I could ever make so great an effort to hide and withstand. I would not care to rate wisdom at so high a price as that. I do not so much look at what that man does, as what it costs him not to do worse.

Another great man boasted to me of the gentle correctness of his manners, which was truly unique. I replied that, especially in one of so eminent a rank and on whom all eyes were turned, it was indeed something to present oneself always moderate to the world, but that the main thing was to provide inwardly for oneself: to my taste a man was not managing his business well if he was eating his insides out. I am afraid that he was doing just that, so as to maintain the mask of that outward appearance of correctness.

By hiding our choler we drive it into our bodies: as Diogenes said to Demosthenes, who kept drawing back further inside so as not to be spotted in a tavern: 'The more you draw back, the further in you go!'[11] I would advise you to give your valet a rather unseasonable slap on the cheek rather than to torture your mind so as to put on an appearance of wisdom; I would rather make

10. Virgil, *Aeneid*, VII, 462–6.
11. Erasmus, *Apophthegmata*, III, *Diogenes Cynicus*, XXXIII.

an exhibition of my passions than brood over them to my cost: express them, vent them, and they grow weaker; it is better to let them jab outside us than be turned against us: '*Omnia vitia in aperto leviora sunt; . . . et tunc perniciosissima cum simulata sanitate subsidunt.*' [All defects are lighter in the open: . . . they are most pernicious when concealed beneath a pretence of soundness.][12]

I advise those of my family who have the right to show their anger, firstly to be sparing of their choler and not to scatter it abroad no matter what the cost, since that thwarts its action and its weight; even the anger you vent on a servant for a theft makes no impression then: it is the same anger he has seen you use against him a hundred times already, for a glass badly rinsed or a stool left out of place. Secondly, let them not get angry in the void; let them see that their reprimand falls to the one they are complaining about, for as a rule they are yelling before he has answered their summons; and they go on doing so for ages after he has gone:

> *et secum petulans amentia certat.*
> [petulant madness turns against itself.][13]

They go at their own shadows and bluster about in places when nobody is punished or affected by it, except such as cannot stand their din.

I similarly blame those who boast and bluster about

12. Seneca, *Epist. moral.*, LVI, 10.
13. Claudianus, *In Eutropium*, I, 237; then Virgil, *Aeneid*, XII, 103–6.

in quarrels where there is no adversary: let them keep such rodomontades for when they can have a target:

> *Mugitus veluti cum prima in prælia taurus*
> *Terrificos ciet atque irasci in cornua tentat,*
> *Arboris obnixus trunco, ventósque lacessit*
> *Ictibus, et sparsa ad pugnam proludit arena.*

[Thus roars the bull fresh to the combat. With terrifying bellows it tries out its anger by dashing its horns against a tree-trunk; it lashes out at the air and paws the sand in the arena as a prelude to battle.]

When I get angry it is as lively, but also as short and as secret, as I can make it. I lose control quickly and violently, but not with such turmoil that I go gaily hurling about all sorts of insults at random and fail to lodge my goads pertinently where I think they can do the most damage: for I normally use only my tongue. My servants get off more cheaply in serious cases than in little ones. The little ones take me by surprise: unfortunately, once you are over the edge, no matter what gave you the shove, you go right down to the bottom; the very fall, of itself, presses on in haste and confusion. In the serious cases I am satisfied with their being so obvious that everybody expects me to give birth to justified anger: I glory in disappointing their expectations. I prepare and brace myself against those serious cases: they dig into my brain and threaten to carry me too far if I follow where they lead. No matter how violent the cause it is easy to prevent myself from giving way to the impulsion of that passion, and I am strong enough to resist it, provided I am expecting it. But if it takes me unawares and once gets a hold on me I am carried away, no matter how trivial the cause.

This is the bargain I strike with those who may have to contend with me: when you see I am the first to get worked up, just let me go on, right or wrong: I will do the same in return. The storm is engendered only by the confluence of cholers, both prone to beget the other: and they are not both born at the same instant. Let us allow each one to run its course: then we always have peace.

A useful prescription but difficult in practice.

It sometimes happens that, without any real emotion, I put on an act of being angry in order to govern my household. But as my age renders my humours more and more acrid I strive to oppose them; if I can, I will see that, from this time forth, the more justification and inclination I have, the less I shall be chagrined and difficult – although I have been among the least so up till now.

One more word to close this chapter. Aristotle says that choler sometimes serves virtue and valour as a weapon.[14] That is most likely; nevertheless those who deny it have an amusing reply: it must be some new-fangled weapon; for we wield the other weapons: that one wields us; it is not our hand that guides it: it guides our hand; it gets a hold on us: not we on it.

14. Aristotle, *Nicomachaean Ethics*, III, viii, 1167b.

# On Virtue

I find from experience that there is a difference between
the leaps and sallies of the soul and a settled constant habit:
and I am well aware that there is nothing we cannot do
(indeed, even surpassing the Divinity, as somebody once
said, since it is a greater thing to make oneself impassible
than to be so as a property of one's being) even combining
the frailty of Man with the resolution and assurance of
God.[1] But only spasmodically. Sometimes there is in the
lives of those heroes in Ancient times miraculous flashes
which appear far to exceed our natural powers: but, truly,
flashes they are; it is hard to believe that we can so steep
and dye our soul in such elevated attributes that they
become ordinary and natural to her. It happens even to us
who are mere abortions of men that we can occasionally
enrapture our Soul far beyond her ordinary state when
she is awakened by the words or examples of another
man: but it is a kind of passion which impels her, disturbs
her and ravishes her somewhat outside ourselves; for
once that whirlwind is over, we can see that she spon-
taneously relaxes and comes down, not perhaps down
to the lowest stage of all but at least to less than she was,
so that we can be moved to anger more or less like any
ordinary man by the loss of a hawk or by a broken glass.

1. Seneca, *Epist. moral.*, LIII, 11–12.

Ordinate conduct, moderation, constancy apart, I believe that anything at all can be done, even by a man who, taken overall, is lacking and deficient. That is why the wise men say that to judge a man properly we must principally look at his routine activities and surprise him in his everyday dress.

Like all other true philosophers, Pyrrho, the man who built up ignorance into so pleasing a science, made an assay at conforming his life to his doctrine. And because he maintained that the feebleness of human judgement was so extreme as to be unable to incline towards any decision or persuasion and wanted to keep it forever hanging in the balance, regarding and welcoming all things as adiaphora, stories are told how he always maintained the same manner and expression: when he had started to say anything he never failed to go on to the end, even if the man he was speaking to had walked off; he never swerved from his path for any obstacle whatsoever, protected only by his friends from precipices or from being bumped into by carts, and similar accidents; for to fear or to avoid anything would have shocked his own principles, which remove all choice and election even from the senses. On occasions he allowed himself to be cut open or cauterized with such steadfastness that he never batted an eyelid.

Now it is one thing to bring your soul to accept such ideas: it is quite another to combine theory and practice. Yet it is not impossible. But what is virtually incredible is that you should combine them with such perseverance and constancy as to make it your regular routine in actions so far from common custom. That is why, when he was once surprised in his home quarrelling bitterly with his sister and reproached for having thereby forgotten his adiaphorism, he retorted: 'What! Must even this silly woman serve to prove my rules?' On another occasion he was seen defending himself against a dog; 'It is,' he said, 'very difficult to cast off the Man entirely, and we must make it our duty to strive to fight against things first by deeds or, as second best, by reason and argument.'[2]

About seven or eight years ago, some two leagues from here, there was a villager, who is still alive; his brain had long been battered by his wife's jealousy; one day he came home from work to be welcomed by her usual nagging; it made him so mad that, taking the sickle he still had in his hand he suddenly lopped off the members which put her into such a fever and chucked them in her face.

It is also told how one of our young local gentry who was desperately in love at last succeeded, by sheer perseverance, in softening the heart of his beautiful lady; he was thrown into despair when about to make his sally to find that it was he who was the soft and yielding one, and that

*non viriliter*
*Iners senile penis extulerat caput;*
[without virility his sluggish penis raised its senile head;][3]

he went straight back home and cut it off, sending it as a cruel and bloody victim to atone for his offence. If that had been done rationally for religion, like the priests of

2. Diogenes Laertius, *Pyrrho*, IX.    3. Tibullus, *De inertia inguinis*.

Cybele, what would we not have said of so sublime an action!

A few days ago at Bergerac, about five leagues up the Dordogne from my house, there was a wife who had been battered and beaten the previous night by her husband, a man melancholic and irritable by complexion; she resolved to escape from his brutality at the cost of her life. She got up and gossiped with her neighbours as usual, slipping in a word or two entrusting her affairs to them; she took a sister of hers by the hand and led her to the bridge; after saying goodbye as though it were a game, with no other shift or change of expression, she threw herself off it down into the river, where she perished. What is more remarkable in her case is that this project had matured in her brain all night long.

It is quite another matter with women in India. It is the custom there for husbands to have several wives and for the one he loves most to kill herself after him: during the whole of their lives they each scheme to gain this vantage point over the others; the kindnesses which they do to their husband aim at no other reward than to be selected to accompany him in death:

> *Ubi mortifero jacta est fax ultima lecto,*
> *Uxorum fusis stat pia turba comis;*
> *Et certamen habent lethi, quæ viva sequatur*
> *Conjugium; pudor est non licuisse mori.*
> *Ardent victrices, et flamme pectora præbent,*
> *Imponuntque suis ora perusta viris.*

[When the last torch is cast on the funeral pyre, the wives remain there with their hair in disarray and begin their mortal combat over which of them, alive, may join their husband in death; for it is a disgrace not to be allowed to die. Those who emerge victorious offer their bosoms to the flames and press their scorched lips on their husband.][4]

One writer says that even in our own times he has seen the custom honoured by those Eastern peoples among whom not only the wives are buried with their husbands but also the slave-girls he had enjoyed. This is the way it is done. When her husband is dead the widow can if she wishes – but few do – ask for two or three months to arrange her affairs. When the day arrives she is arrayed as for a wedding, a looking-glass in her left hand and a wand in the other; she mounts a horse and with a happy face as though, she says, she were going to lie asleep beside her husband. Having paraded in pomp accompanied by her friends and relations and by a crowd in festive mood, she eventually comes to a public place devoted to such spectacles – a great square in the midst of which is a ditch filled with wood, having next to it a mound four or five steps high on to which she is escorted where she is served a sumptuous repast. After which she begins to dance and to sing; when the moment seems right to her she commands that the fire be lit. That done, she comes down and, taking her husband's nearest kinsman by the hand, they go together to the neighbouring river where she strips herself naked, distributes her clothes and jewels among her friends and plunges into the water as though to lave away her sins. She comes

4. Propertius, II, xiii, 17–22.

out and wraps herself in a yellow cloth fourteen yards long; then, again offering her hand to her husband's kinsman, they return to the mound from which she addresses the people and, if she has any, entrusts her children to their care. Between the ditch and the mound they are willing to draw a curtain to hide that burning furnace from her view; many widows forbid them to do so, to show greater courage. When she has finished what she has to say, a woman presents her with a cruse of oil to anoint her head and her whole body; after having done so, she casts it into the fire and then immediately leaps in herself, whereupon the people throw a great many faggots on top of her to save her from a lingering death; then their joy turns to mourning and sadness. If they are people of meaner stuff the dead body of the husband is taken to the spot where it is to be buried; there it is placed in a sitting position; the widow kneels before it and embraces it tightly. She remains in that posture while they build a wall around them; when it reaches just up to the widow's shoulders, one of her family grabs her head from behind and twists her neck; once her spirit has departed the wall is quickly raised and covered over and there they remain entombed.

In that same country there was a similar practice among their Gymnosophists for, not by the constraint of others nor by a sudden caprice but by the express terms of their profession, their custom was, as they were approaching a certain age or realized that they were threatened by some disease, to have a pyre built for them, on top of which was placed a bed richly adorned;

then, after having joyfully feasted their friends and acquaintances, they settled themselves firmly on that bed, resolved that when the fire was put to it no man should see them stir hand or foot. Thus did one of them, Calanus, die before the entire army of Alexander the Great.[5] And no man among them was reckoned holy or blessed unless he killed himself that way, having dispatched his soul, purged and purified by fire, after all that was mortal and earthy in him had been consumed.

What makes it a miracle is that stable, lifelong premeditation. For intermingled with it is, among our other debates, the question of fate, FATUM. For if we bind things to come and our very wills to a definite and inevitable necessity, we are still on that age-old argument: since God foresees, as he undoubtedly does, that all must happen thus, happen thus they must. To which *Magistri Nostri* reply that to see something happen as we do – and God, too (since all is present to him; he sees rather than foresees) – is not to force it to happen. Indeed, we see the things because they happen: they do not happen because we see them. The event produces the knowledge, not the knowledge the event. What we see happen *is* happening: but it could have happened otherwise. And God, in the book of the causes of events which he has in his foreknowledge, also includes such causes as we term fortuitous and voluntary, those which depend on the liberty which he has given to our free-will: he knows that we will go astray because we shall have

5. Plutarch, *Life of Alexander*.

willed to do so. Now I have seen plenty of nations encouraging their troops with this necessity of Fate. For if our hour is bound to come at a particular point, neither volleys from enemy harquebuses nor our own rashness nor our running away nor our cowardice can advance it or retard it. That is a beautiful saying: but find a man who will act on it! And if it is the case that a strong and lively belief brings in its train analogous actions, then that faith which our mouths are so full of is wondrously light in our own age, unless it be that her contempt for works makes her despise their company! All the same, while on this subject, the Sire de Joinville, as good a witness as any other, tells us that the Bedouin, a people living among the Saracens with whom our King Saint Louis had some trouble in the Holy Land, believe so firmly by their religion that the days of each man have been numbered in advance by a preordained inevitability that they go bare to the wars except for a sword of Turkish fashion and a white linen garment. And the worst malediction they always had on their lips when they were angry with one of their own men was, 'Cursed be thou like he who wears armour for fear of death!' That is a very different proof of belief and faith than ours is.[6]

We can rank with it the proof given by two monks of Florence in the time of our fathers. Opposed over some point of doctrine they agreed that both of them should be burned in the public square before all the people, each one wishing to prove he was right. All the prep-

6. Joinville, *Vie de Saint Louis*, XXX.

arations had been made and the deed on the very point of being done when it was interrupted by some unforeseen incident.

A young Turkish lord had personally performed some remarkable feat of arms before the armies of both Amurath and Hunyadi who were ready to join battle; when Amurath asked him how a youth so young and inexperienced (for it was the first war he had seen) had been filled with such noble and valliant courage, he replied that his sovereign tutor in valour had been a hare. 'I was out hunting one day,' he said, 'when I came across a hare lying in its form; although I had two excellent greyhounds at my side it seemed to me better, so as not to lose it, to use my bow, for it made a very good target. I started shooting off my arrows – I had some forty odd in my quiver – but did not hit it, let alone disturb it. In the end I let loose my hounds: they could do nothing either. This made me realize that that hare was protected by destiny and that swords or arrows only strike home by leave of our fate, which it is not in our power to retard or advance.'

That tale should teach us *en passant* how bendable our reason is to all sorts of conceptions. A man of importance, great in years, in glory, in dignity and in doctrine, boasted to me that he had been led to make a most important change of faith by some monition coming to him, one so bizarre and incidentally so inconclusive that I found that it tended, rather, the opposite way. He called it a miracle. So did I – in a different sense.

The historians of the Turks say that this conviction that their days are numbered by the unbending decision of Fate is so widespread among the people that it manifestly is seen to give them assurance in danger. And I know a great Prince who may nobly draw some profit from it, if Fortune continues to give him a shove.[7]

In living memory there has been seen no more strikingly resolute act than that of the two men who plotted the death of the Prince of Orange. It is a marvel how anyone could have so enflamed the second of them, who brought it off, for an undertaking in which his comrade had fared so badly despite doing all that he could: to go and follow in his tracks, and with the same weapons to take on a nobleman, freshly armed with a lesson in mistrust and strong in bodily strength and in his retinue of friends, in his own hall, surrounded by his guards, and in a town devoted to him! He indeed had brought to bear a most determined hand and a mind moved by a stalwart passion. A dagger is surer to land a blow; but since it requires a bigger movement and more strength of arm than does a pistol, its blow is more susceptible to being warded off or intercepted. I have no great doubt that that man knew he was running to a certain death: for any hopes which he could have been brought to entertain could find no lodging in a settled intelligence – and the way he executed his deed shows that he had no lack of that, no more than of courage.

The motives for such a powerful conviction may well be various, since our faculty of perception does with us, and with itself, whatever it likes.

7. Doubtless Henry of Navarre (Henry IV).

That other assassination carried out near Orleans was nothing like it: there was far more chance in it than vigour; the blow itself would not have been fatal if chance had not rendered it so; and the design of shooting from the saddle, and at a distance, and at a man who was jogging up and down with his horse, was the plan of a man who would rather lose his chance than lose his life. What happened afterwards proves this. For the thought of having killed someone so exalted made him dazed and transfixed so that he completely lost his wits and was too disturbed to guard his escape, or his tongue under questioning. What did he have to do, beyond galloping back to his friends across a river! It is a method I have leapt to in lesser dangers and which I do not consider very hazardous, however wide the crossing, provided that your horse readily finds its footing and you can see ahead to an easy place to land on the other side, depending on the current. As for that other man,[8] when they pronounced his dreadful sentence, he replied, 'I was ready for that: I will amaze you by my endurance.'

The Assassins, who are a people dependent on Phoenicia, are considered by the Mahometans to be sovereignly devout and pure in morals. They hold that the surest way to merit paradise is to kill someone of an opposing religion. They therefore show contempt for all personal danger and are often to be found singly or in pairs, carrying out such profitable executions at the cost of their certain death, appearing before an enemy

8. Balthasar Gérard.

in the midst of his troops to 'assassinate' him – (it is from them that we have borrowed that word). Our own Count Raymond of Tripoli was killed this way in his own city.

# On Sleep

Reason ordains that we should keep to the same road but not to the same rate; and although the wise man must never allow his human passions to make him stray from the right path, he may without prejudice to his duty certainly quicken or lessen his speed, though never plant himself down like some fixed and impassive Colossus. If Virtue herself were incarnate I believe that even her pulse would beat faster when attacking the foe than when attacking a dinner – indeed it is necessary that she should be moved and inflamed. That is why I have noted as something quite rare the sight of great persons who remain so utterly unmoved when engaged in high enterprises and in affairs of some moment that they do not even cut short their sleep.

On the day appointed for his desperate battle against Darius, Alexander the Great slept so soundly and so late that when the hour of battle was pressing close, Parmenion was obliged to enter his chamber and call out his name two or three times to wake him up.[1]

The very same night that the Emperor Otho had resolved to end his life, he put his private affairs in order, distributed his money between his followers, sharpened the edge of the sword he intended to use for his blow

1. Cf. Erasmus, *Apophthegmata*, VI, *Alexander Magnus*, LXIV.

and then, waiting only to know that each one of his friends had withdrawn to safety, fell so soundly asleep that his servants of the bedchamber heard him snoring.

The death of that Emperor has much in common with the death of the great Cato, and especially that feature; for when Cato was ready to take his own life, he was waiting for news to be brought that the Senators he had sent away had sailed out of the port of Utica when he fell into so deep a sleep that his breathing could be heard in the neighbouring room; and when the man he had sent to the port woke him to tell him of the storm which had prevented the Senators from sailing away in safety, he dispatched another and, settling down in his bed, he went off to sleep again until the man came back and told him that they had left.

And we can again compare him to Alexander, when during the Catiline Conspiracy there was such a storm over the treachery of Metellus the tribune who was determined to publish the decree summoning Pompey and his army back to Rome. Cato alone opposed that decree and he and Metellus had exchanged gross insults and great threats in the Senate; but the decision had to be carried out the following morning in the public Forum. Metellus was to come there, favoured by the plebs as well as by Caesar who was then allied to Pompey's interests: he was to be accompanied by a crowd of foreign mercenaries and gladiators who would fight to the last; Cato was to come supported by nothing but his own constancy. His family and friends and many others were deeply anxious about this: some of them spent the night together with no desire to sleep, drink or eat because of the danger they saw awaiting him; his wife and his sisters especially did nothing but fill his home with weeping and wailing; he on the contrary reassured everyone there; having dined as usual, he went to lie down and slept a deep sleep until morning, when one of his fellow tribunes came to wake him up to enter the affray. What we know of the courage of this man from the rest of his life enables us to judge with absolute certainty that what he did proceeded from a soul high above such events, which he did not deign to take to heart more than any ordinary occurrence.

In that sea-fight which Augustus won against Sextus Pompeius off Sicily, he was just about to go into battle when he was overcome by so sound a sleep that his friends had to come and wake him up to get him to give the signal for the engagement. That provided Mark Antony later on with an excuse for accusing him of not having the will even to look straight in the eye of the troops he had drawn up for battle and of not daring to face his soldiers before Agrippa came to tell him the news of his own victory over his enemies.

But to turn to young Marius, he did worse: for on the day of his last encounter with Sylla, he drew up his army, gave the signal for battle, then went to lie down for a rest in the shade of a tree where he fell so fast asleep that he could scarcely be awakened by the rout of his fleeing soldiers, having seen nothing of the combat; they say it was from being so exhausted by fatigue and want of sleep that nature could stand no more.

While on this topic it is for the doctors to decide whether sleep is such a necessity that our very life depends on it: for we are certainly told that King Perseus of Macedonia, when a prisoner in Rome, was done to death by being prevented from sleeping.

Herodotus mentions nations where men sleep and wake a half-year at a time. And the biographer of Epimenides the Wise says that he slept for fifty-seven years in a row.[2]

2. Herodotus, *History*, IV, xxv; Diogenes Laertius, *Life of Epimenides*.

# On the Length of Life

I cannot accept the way we determine the span of our lives. I note that wise men shorten it considerably compared to the common opinion. 'What!' said Cato the Younger to those who wanted to stop him killing himself: 'Am I still at the age when you can accuse me of leaving life too soon?'[1] Yet he was only forty-eight. He reckoned, considering how few men reach it, that his age was fully mature and well advanced. And those who keep themselves going with the thought that some span of life or other which they call 'natural' promises them a few years more could only do so provided that there was some ordinance exempting them personally from those innumerable accidents (which each one of us comes up against and is subject to by nature) which can rupture the course of life which they promise themselves.

What madness it is to expect to die of that failing of our powers brought on by extreme old age and to make that the target for our life to reach when it is the least usual, the rarest kind of death. We call that death, alone, a natural death, as if it were unnatural to find a man breaking his neck in a fall, engulfed in a shipwreck, surprised by plague or pleurisy, and as though our normal condition did not expose us to all of those harms.

1. Plutarch, *Life of Cato of Utica*.

Let us not beguile ourselves with such fine words: perhaps we ought, rather, to call natural anything which is generic, common to all and universal. Dying of old age is a rare death, unique and out of the normal order and therefore less natural than the others. It is the last, the uttermost way of dying; the farther it is from us, the less we can hope to reach it; it is indeed the limit beyond which we shall not go and which has been prescribed by Nature's law as never to be crossed: but it is a very rare individual law of hers which makes us last out till then. It is an exemption which she grants as an individual favour to one man in the space of two or three centuries, freeing him from the burden of those obstacles and difficulties which she strews along the course of that long progress.

Therefore my opinion is that we should consider whatever age we have reached as an age reached by few. Since in the normal course of events men never reach that far, it is a sign that we are getting on. And since we have crossed the accustomed limits – and that constitutes the real measure of our days – we ought not to hope to get much farther beyond them; having escaped those many occasions of death which have tripped up all the others, we ought to admit that an abnormal fortune such as that which has brought us so far is indeed beyond the usual procedure and cannot last much longer.

It is a defect in our very laws to hold that false idea, for they do not admit that a man be capable of managing his affairs before the age of twenty-five, yet he can scarcely manage to make his life last that long! Augustus lopped five years off the old Roman ordinances and decreed that it sufficed to be thirty for a man to assume the office of judge. Servius Tullius exempted knights who had passed the age of forty-seven from obligatory war-service; Augustus remitted it at forty-five.[2] Sending men into inactivity before fifty-five or sixty does not seem very right to me. I would counsel extending our vocations and employments as far as we could in the public interest; the error is on the other side, I find: that of not putting us to work soon enough. The man who had power to decide everything in the whole world at nineteen[3] wanted a man to be thirty before he could decide where to place a gutter!

Personally I reckon that our souls are free from their bonds at the age of twenty, as they ought to be, and that by then they show promise of all they are capable of. No soul having failed by then to give a quite evident pledge of her power ever gave proof of it afterwards. By then – or never at all – natural qualities and capacities reveal whatever beauty or vigour they possess.

> *Si l'espine nou pique quand nai,*
> *A peine que pique jamai*
> [If a thorn pricks not at its birth,
> It will hardly prick at all]

as they say in Dauphiné.

Of all the fair deeds of men in ancient times and in our own which have come to my knowledge, of whatever kind they may be, I think it would take me longer

2. Suetonius, *Life of Augustus*.     3. The Emperor Augustus.

to enumerate those which were made manifest before the age of thirty than after. Yes, and often in the lives of the very same men: may I not say that with total certainty in the case of Hannibal and his great adversary Scipio? They lived a good half of their lives on the glory achieved in their youth: they were great men later compared with others, but not great compared with themselves. As for me, I am convinced that, since that age, my mind and my body have not grown but diminished, and have retreated not advanced.

It may well be that (for those who make good use of their time) knowledge and experience grow with the years but vitality, quickness, firmness and other qualities which are more truly our own, and more important, more ours by their essence, droop and fade.

> *Ubi jam validis quassatum est viribus ævi*
> *Corpus, et obtusis ceciderunt viribus artus,*
> *Claudicat ingenium, delirat linguaque mensque.*

[When the body is shattered by the mighty blows of age and our limbs shed their blunted powers, our wits too become lame and our tongues and our minds start to wander.][4]

Sometimes it is the body which is the first to surrender to old age, sometimes too the soul; and I have known plenty of men whose brains grew weak before their stomachs or their legs; and it is all the more dangerous an infirmity in that the sufferer is hardly aware of it and its symptoms are not clear ones.

4. Lucretius, III, 452–4.

But now I am complaining not that the laws allow us to work so late but that they are so late in putting us to work.

It seems to me that, considering the frailty of our life and the number of natural hazards to which it is exposed, we should not allow so large a place in it to being born, to leisure and to our apprenticeship.

# How we Weep and Laugh at the Same Thing

When we read in our history books that Antigonus was severely displeased with his son for having brought him the head of his enemy King Pyrrhus who had just been killed fighting against him and that he burst into copious tears when he saw it,[1] and that Duke René of Lorraine also lamented the death of Duke Charles of Burgundy whom he had just defeated, and wore mourning at his funeral; and that at the battle of Auroy which the Count de Montfort won against Charles de Blois, his rival for the Duchy of Brittany, the victor showed great grief when he happened upon his enemy's corpse: we should not at once exclaim,

> Et cosi aven che l'animo ciascuna
> Sua passion sotto et contrario manto
> Ricopre, con la vista hor' chiara hor bruna.

[Thus does the mind cloak every passion with its opposite, our faces showing now joy, now sadness.][2]

When they presented Caesar with the head of Pompey our histories say[3] that he turned his gaze away as from a spectacle both ugly and displeasing. There had been

---

1. Plutarch, *Life of Pyrrhus*.    2. Petrarch, Sonnet 81.
3. Plutarch, *Life of Caesar*.

such a long understanding and fellowship between them in the management of affairs of State, they had shared the same fortunes and rendered each other so many mutual services as allies, that we should not believe that his behaviour was quite false and counterfeit – as this other poet thinks it was:

> *tutumque putavit*
> *Jam bonus esse socer; lachrimas non sponte cadentes*
> *Effudit, gemitusque expressit pectore læto.*

[And now he thought it was safe to play the good father-in-law; he poured out tears, but not spontaneous ones, and he forced out groans from his happy breast.]⁴

For while it is true that most of our actions are but mask and cosmetic, and that it is sometimes true that

> *Hæredis fletus sub persona risus est;*
> [Behind the mask, the tears of an heir are laughter;]⁵

nevertheless we ought to consider when judging such events how our souls are often shaken by conflicting emotions. Even as there is said to be a variety of humours assembled in our bodies, the dominant one being that which normally prevails according to our complexion, so too in our souls: although diverse emotions may shake them, there is one which must remain in possession of the field; nevertheless its victory is not so complete

4. Lucan, *Pharsalia*, 1037–9.
5. Publius Syrus *apud* Aulus Gellius, XVII, 14.

but that the weaker ones do not sometimes regain lost ground because of the pliancy and mutability of our soul and make a brief sally in their turn. That is why we can see that not only children, who artlessly follow Nature, often weep and laugh at the same thing, but that not one of us either can boast that, no matter how much he may want to set out on a journey, he still does not feel his heart a-tremble when he says goodbye to family and friends: even if he does not actually burst into tears at least he puts foot to stirrup with a sad and gloomy face. And however noble the passion which enflames the heart of a well-born bride, she still has to have her arms prised from her mother's neck before being given to her husband, no matter what that merry fellow may say:

> *Est ne novis nuptis odio venus, anne parentum*
> *Frustrantur falsis gaudia lachrimulis,*
> *Ubertim thalami quas intra limina fundunt?*
> *Non, ita me divi, vera gemunt, juverint.*

[Is Venus really hated by our brides, or do they mock their parents' joy with those false tears which they pour forth in abundance at their chamber-door? No. So help me, gods, their sobs are false ones.][6]

And so it is not odd to lament the death of a man whom we would by no means wish to be still alive.

When I rail at my manservant I do so sincerely with all my mind: my curses are real not feigned. But once I cease to fume, if he needs help from me I am glad to

6. Catullus, *De coma Berenices*, LXVI, 15.

help him: I turn over the page. When I call him a dolt
or a calf I have no intention of stitching such labels on
to him for ever: nor do I believe I am contradicting
myself when I later call him an honest fellow. No one
characteristic clasps us purely and universally in its
embrace. If only talking to oneself did not look mad, no
day would go by without my being heard growling to
myself, against myself, 'You silly shit!' Yet I do not intend
that to be a definition of me.

If anyone should think when he sees me sometimes
look bleakly at my wife and sometimes lovingly that
either emotion is put on, then he is daft. When Nero
took leave of his mother whom he was sending to
be drowned, he nevertheless felt some emotion at his
mother's departure and felt horror and pity.

The sun, they say, does not shed its light in one
continuous flow but ceaselessly darts fresh rays so thickly
at us, one after another, that we cannot perceive any gap
between them:

> *Largus enim liquidi fons luminis, ætherius sol*
> *Inrigat assidue cælum candore recenti,*
> *Suppeditatque novo confestim lumine lumen.*

[That generous source of liquid light, the aethereal sun, assidu-
ously floods the heavens with new rays and ceaselessly sheds
light upon new light.][7]

So, too, our soul darts its arrows separately but imperceptibly.

7. Lucretius, V, 282–4.

Artabanus happened to take his nephew Xerxes by surprise. He teased him about the sudden change which he saw come over his face. But Xerxes was in fact thinking about the huge size of his army as it was crossing the Hellespont for the expedition against Greece; he first felt a quiver of joy at seeing so many thousands of men devoted to his service and showed this by a happy and festive look on his face; then, all of a sudden his thoughts turned to all those lives which would wither in a hundred years at most: he knit his brow and was saddened to tears.[8]

We have pursued revenge for an injury with a resolute will; we have felt a singular joy at our victory . . . and we weep: yet it is not for that that we weep. Nothing has changed; but our mind contemplates the matter in a different light and sees it from another aspect: for everything has many angles and many different sheens. Thoughts of kinship, old acquaintanceships and affections suddenly seize our minds and stir them each according to their worth: but the change is so sudden that it escapes us:

> *Nil adeo fieri celeri ratione videtur*
> *Quam si mens fieri proponit et inchoat ipsa.*
> *Ocius ergo animus quam res se perciet ulla,*
> *Ante oculos quarum in promptu natura videtur.*

[Nothing can be seen to match the rapidity of the thoughts which the mind produces and initiates. The mind is swifter than anything which the nature of our eyes allows them to see.][9]

8. After Herodotus, VII, xlv, and Valerius Maximus, IX, xiii.
9. Lucretius, III, 183–6.

That is why we deceive ourselves if we want to make this neverending succession into one continuous whole. When Timoleon weeps for the murder which, with noble determination, he committed, he does not weep for the liberty he has restored to his country; he does not weep for the Tyrant: he weeps for his brother.[10] He has done one part of his duty: let us allow him to do the other.

10. Plutarch, *Life of Timoleon*.